Contents

INTRODUCTION

THE JOURNEY AHEAD

Welcome to an investigative endeavor that critically reevaluates established notions concerning North American history. The book you hold challenges mainstream views and sometimes even disproves the historical record as we know it.

We began studying the first maps covering North America, and one of our first observations drew us into California and the San Francisco Bay. An odd detail on a map opened a new set of questions and discoveries we felt we had to explore further. Imagine a sweater with one loose thread. When you pull that thread, the whole sweater starts to come apart, revealing what it is really made of. That happened to us with this one detail on several ancient maps.

We quickly found that our research and analysis needed to balance complex information. We used three tentpoles in our inquiry: Occam's Razor, syntopical analysis, and a model based on means, motive, and opportunity.

Occam's Razor is a principle that suggests more straightforward explanations are usually better than complex ones. This helped us initially, but we needed a more complete method as our research deepened. That is where syntopical analysis came in. This meant looking at many topics and organizing the ideas and data within them to understand isolated events over the broader landscapes of world events. It helped us see connections between things that seemed unrelated at first. The third methodology was the standard of means, motive, and opportunity. This method analyzed what happened, when, why, who it happened to, and how it was done.

The chapters ahead will walk you through our research findings step by step.

We are not just trying to replace one story with another.

We want to make history accurate and backed up by solid evidence.

We invite you to engage with us in this rigorous intellectual expedition that paves the way for a more comprehensive, albeit unsettling, grasp of history and its multifarious interpretations.

Jon Levi

David Edward

CHAPTER 1: MAPS WITH GAPS

STARTING TO SPOT THE PLOT

THE NAMING OF SAN FRANCISCO

California's history is well documented.

Juan Rodríguez Cabrillo, a Portuguese explorer sailing for the Spanish Crown, was the first European who deeply explored the California coast. He embarked on his voyage in 1542, departing from the port of Navidad in modern-day Mexico. Cabrillo explored much of the California coastline but did not venture far inland. He named various features along the coast, including San Miguel Island (Bancroft, 1885).

However, most of the names we use for California locations today came after Cabrillo. A good example is San Francisco and San Francisco Bay, which were discovered, we are told, over two centuries later. Gaspar de Portolà, a Spanish military officer and explorer, and his overland expedition revealed the area in 1769 (Paddison, 1999; Starr, 2005).

Gaspar de Portolà had been appointed to govern both Baja (Lower) California and Alta (Upper) California in 1767. During his tenure as governor, he oversaw Spanish territories in the region and ensured the success of their colonization efforts. His appointment as governor was part of Spain's broader strategy to consolidate and strengthen its control over its North American territories. Two years into his appointment, this role led him to spearhead the expedition to explore and establish missions in Alta, California, eventually discovering San Francisco Bay.

Gaspar de Portolà

This momentous discovery was not just a footnote in history books; it came alive in the detailed expedition diaries. Specifically, Herbert Ingram Priestley's translation of Father Juan Crespi's accounts gives us a firsthand look into their adventurous journey and the exhilaration of their find (Portolà, 1769/1938).

History tells us that San Francisco Bay was named by Spanish explorers in honor of St. Francis of Assisi. Specifically, it was the Spanish explorer and naval officer Juan Manuel de Ayala who, in 1775, charted the entrance to the bay and named it "La Boca del Puerto de San Francisco" or "The Mouth of the Port of San Francisco" (Lightfoot & Parrish, 2009).

The name was fitting since the nearby mission, established by Father Junípero Serra a year later in 1776, was named "Mission San Francisco de Asís," which also honored St. Francis of Assisi (Starr, 2005). Over time, the name "San Francisco" became associated with the bay, the surrounding area, and eventually the city itself.

THE PROBLEM WITH SAN FRANCISCO

The prior account is undisputed in American history. It is drawn from multiple well-established, peer-reviewed books and articles, including works sympathetic to indigenous populations like Lightfoot (2009). It is a story that has consistently been repeated as true as far back as Portolà's (1769) journal, Bancroft's (1885) history, and into modern times with examples like Paddison (1999) and Starr (2005).

The challenge is that this story isn't even close to accurate.

1669 Map "Amerique Septentrionale"

In 17th-century France, the craft of map-making wasn't just a scholarly endeavor but a matter of professional pride and economic survival. Central to this era's cartographic achievements is the 1669 map "Amerique Septentrionale." Guillaume Sanson, responsible for its design, was deeply influenced by the legacy of his father, Nicolas Sanson, often regarded as a trailblazer in French cartography. Guillaume, upholding the Sanson reputation, knew that his livelihood and stature hinged on the precision and detail of his maps (Pastoureau, 1984).

Working in parallel, Pierre Mariette, a top-tier Parisian print dealer, ensured that these meticulously crafted maps reached a broad audience. His family name, synonymous with quality in the print world, also demanded the utmost accuracy in the items they dealt with, which included collaborations with skilled mapmakers like Sanson (Préaud et al., 1987). The production and distribution of the "Amerique Septentrional" map were not mere routine tasks for Sanson and Mariette. Their reputations and livelihoods were on the line, making the map a reflection of geographical knowledge and a testament to their unwavering commitment to accuracy and quality.

The Amerique Septentrionale map, printed almost one hundred years before the discovery of San Francisco Bay in 1769, contradicts the story that San Francisco was named after the nearby Mission San Francisco de Asís, itself founded *107 years after the map was printed.*

1669 Map "Amerique Septentrionale" showing S. Francisco

The map contains the label S. Francisco along the California coast, in a bay.

How could this be possible?

There is not a direct or known link between "S. Francisco" and any pre-Columbian Native American cultures or traditions (at least none that we have uncovered in our extensive research). Pre-Columbian societies had their own names and identifiers for their territories, which were different from the names the Spanish and other European colonizers later introduced.

The 1669 map suggests the current historical naming narrative is suspect.

S. Francisco, as a place located in California, was apparently known over a century before its *discovery* by Juan Manuel de Ayala (et al.). The name San Francisco could not have been based on a Spanish 1776 monastery dedicated to St. Francis of Assisi. It is impossible, even though that is the official history we have. We have the name on a map from 1669. The Monastery's founders were not yet born. The men who found the bay were not yet born. We are told the bay had been missed on every prior exploration and mapping exercise until Juan Manuel de Ayala discovered it in 1769.

To solve this 100-year discrepancy, the best interpretation, to our thinking, is that the history might be the other way around; the name San Francisco might have been taken from whatever was presented near current-day San Francisco back in the 16th century and then adopted by the new people moving into the region.

It is Occam's Razor's answer, the most straightforward path; we can delve into a web of assumptions about how speculative or uninformed the cartographers of the time were—questioning their handling of toponyms, projecting incompetence onto an entire industry predicated on professionalism, and demeaning historical figures—or, with simple clarity, we accept the change in the sequencing of San Francisco's toponym (a toponym is the study of the name given to a specific place or geographic location).

Does a change in the toponym for one place change world history?

No, not yet. One map does not change history.

We believe that our findings on the map could lead to a reexamination or revision of our history.

This is no shocking situation; revisions happen all the time. In the 1970s, the prevailing science was that the earth was cooling (Kukla & Kukla, 1972; Rasool & Schneider, 1971). In the 1990s, the prevailing science was that the planet was warming (Hansen et al., 1984; IPCC, 1990).

It was widely believed that slaves constructed the Great Pyramids of Egypt; however, recent archaeological findings suggest they were built by well-fed laborers engaged in state-sponsored labor or community service (Hawass & Lehner, 1997; Redford, 1992).

It was long assumed that Christopher Columbus discovered America, but modern understandings recognize that Vikings, led by Leif Erikson, had reached North American shores around 500 years earlier (Jones, G., 1986; Seaver et al., 1996).

For many years, the city of Troy, as depicted in Homer's "Iliad," was considered a mere legend; however, archaeological excavations by Heinrich Schliemann in the late 19th century uncovered the ruins of this ancient city, validating its historical existence (Schliemann, H., 1881; Easton et al., 1999).

The common belief is that settled farming during the Neolithic era led to religion and complex societies. However, Göbekli Tepe in Turkey, from the end of the Younger Dryas period, disrupted this idea. Its elaborate stone structures suggest that it was built by nomadic hunter-gatherers, indicating that organized religious practices might have begun even before the advent of settled farming (Schmidt, K., 2000; Peters & Schmidt, 2004).

Given history changes, we have a legitimate mystery worth exploring here. More significant revelations have started with lesser findings than ours.

How could the name of one of America's largest and very well-known cities be on a Spanish map a century before the geography's (the bay's) discovery? Much less the founding of the city in 1776?

What would that even mean?

How can we move our finding from suspicion to something more concrete?

S. Francisco has straightforward and specific ties to known historical figures. This is important as it suggests that while the current narrative is inaccurate, the context of the data still falls within some semblance of established mainstream history. It is still a relevant cultural reference. This is because St. Francis of Assisi has his own accepted historical narrative known to us and the day's map makers and explorers.

Saint Francis of Assisi was born in the Umbrian town of Assisi, Italy, around 1181 or 1182 (Englebert, 1965). As the son of a wealthy cloth merchant, Francis enjoyed a lavish early life but underwent a spiritual transformation after experiencing the horrors of war and sickness (Englebert, 1965). This change led him to renounce his inheritance and adopt a life of poverty and piety. He founded the Order of Friars Minor, commonly known as the Franciscans, a religious order emphasizing humility, poverty, and a deep connection with nature.

Francis is often depicted with animals, highlighting his belief in the unity of all creation (Englebert, 1965). His dedication to the poor and appreciation for the natural world left an indelible mark on Christianity. Francis was canonized as a saint by Pope Gregory IX in 1228, only two years after his death. His influence has persisted through the centuries, with millions venerating him as the patron saint of animals and the environment (Englebert, 1965).

Examining the etymology of San Francisco's name sheds light on a multifaceted historical narrative, one intricately interwoven with historical documents from different origins. This seems like a persistent trend, where records from different control systems show different narratives, some directly contrasting others.

While conventionally attributed to Spanish explorers and Mission San Francisco de Asís' establishment, our 1669 map "Amerique Septentrionale" analysis introduces a thought-provoking anomaly. The presence of "S. Francisco" on this map, preceding the established timeline, necessitates a thorough and comprehensive reevaluation of established historical narratives on a broader canvas.

Uncovering hidden irregularities is like casting a wide net into the past. This process pushes us to study old archives and question known ideas. Through this, we go beyond just names and find deeper meanings in history. We used to think the city's name came from Spanish explorers and their missions, but now we see "S. Francisco" existed before that. This new finding encourages us to study history more carefully and enthusiastically.

So, let us do exactly that.

If this map is some one-off anomaly, it is not quite as strong a case as we claim. It begs the question, are there earlier maps with this reference? Even better, how about an earlier map that uses the full name of San Francisco on the California shores instead of S. Francisco?

If it exists, this additional evidence would undoubtedly aid our assertion and provide a compelling reason to research this history.

Urbano Monte's 1587 Map

1587 URBANO MONTE MAP

Urbano Monte's 1587 map is more than a cartographic achievement: it is a window into the Renaissance's worldview. Hailing from Milan, Monte was a man of vision and detail, and his map captures this essence (Van Duzer, 2018). Comprising a vast 60 sheets, when assembled, it stands as one of the most extensive known world maps from the period.

One of the map's distinct features is its polar projection, a unique advanced approach for the period. In constructing this map, Monte meticulously incorporated both documented and geographical knowledge.

Urbano Monte's 1587 Map showing San Francisco

The label "San Francisco" caught our attention in our examination of Monte's map. It is in the same coastal region in what would become California. This mention predates the recognized European discovery of the San Francisco Bay in California by a period of close to two hundred years.

That is a long time.

Monte's 1587 world map is closer in time to Columbus's 1492 voyage (95 years) than to the 1775 discovery of San Francisco Bay (188 years later). Our intrigue deepened upon finding a comparable historic inconsistency on the 1669 map by Guillaume Sanson and Pierre Mariette.

A compelling point emerges when this discovery from Monte's map is juxtaposed against the reference to "S. Francisco" on the 1669 "Amerique Septentrionale" map. The repetition of this name across two independent sources separated by nearly a century challenges the established timelines and possibly emphasizes the layered complexity of historical cartography. Together, these maps prompt a profound reevaluation, suggesting that the name "San Francisco" had roots in the cartographic consciousness well before its conventional association with California.

However, is this the only North American oddity on the 1587 map? No, it is not. The map is littered with depictions of cities throughout North America.

Urbano Monte's 1587 Map showing Tents

Specific illustrations seem consistent with 16th-century Spanish depictions of makeshift structures and permanent settlements. Such sketches depict the use of basic and temporary materials, which is consistent with the portrayal of Native American communities in historical accounts from that era.

Urbano Monte's 1587 Map Showing Cities

Oddly, others are depicted (above image) as cities surrounded by a wall or barrier. In the above image, we can see three such depictions. Alboseda is even more interesting as the tops of the buildings seem to be adorned with something akin to modern-day antennas. We are not proposing a modern-day solution, but we are identifying the characteristic as different from many of the other depictions of cities without antennas, as seen in the image of Cannarian and Ancon, the two cities depicted to the south of Alboseda.

What are all of these cities? There are four or five dozen of them in what is today the US and Canada on this map.

If we see modern names dating back hundreds of years before the history we have for them, and we see the substantive development of the American interior centuries before we are told it was developed, what else is there to find on these old maps?

Can we go back to even earlier maps to make sense of this?

TYPVS ORBIS TERRARVM 1570

Moving still backward in time, we have arguably the first attempt to cite sources for a global map. Abraham Ortelius, a Flemish cartographer, introduced the "Typus Orbis Terrarum" as part of his pioneering atlas, "Theatrum Orbis Terrarum" or "Theatre of the World" (Harley and Woodward, The History of Cartography, 1987). This atlas marked a significant departure from previous map compilations due to its standardized format, including the latest geographic information, and Ortelius's practice of providing citations for his sources (Van den Broecke, 1996).

A comparative analysis between Ortelius and Monte reveals distinct differences in their approach, even though they are only separated by a dozen or so years. Ortelius's work was more compact, formatted for broader distribution, and aimed to synthesize diverse sources of geographic knowledge into a cohesive whole. While equally informed by available sources, Monte's effort leaned towards grandeur, evident in its sheer scale and detailed content. His inclusion of regions like Japan, based on accounts from Jesuit missionaries, underscores this comprehensive approach (Bagrow, 1964).

Typvs Orbis Terrarvm 1570

Both Ortelius and Monte worked with the primary goal of enhancing the contemporary understanding of the world. Their works exemplify the Renaissance spirit, combining rigorous empirical data with intricate design. Commonalities between Ortelius's and Monte's works are undeniable. In essence, while divergent in form and presentation, both maps played foundational roles in the trajectory of modern cartography.

Both maps show dozens of cities in North America, many with the aforementioned antenna or spires, for lack of a more developed term. As noted earlier, the maps display a variety of structures. Some depict a lower infrastructure level, while others show a more complex type of building. These indications show dozens of major and minor cities in the western North American continent at times when there is no historical record of such communities.

What about other regional North American maps from the same relative time period? Are there any material discrepancies found on maps with less scope?

THE MYSTERY OF ROANOKE 1587

Our detective work so far has pushed us all the way back into the late 16th century. It is easy to forget how long ago this was in relation to the maturation of North America. For example, the conditions were still very primitive from a European settlement perspective. New settlements struggled greatly between the harsh, primitive conditions and the mixed socio-political relationships with the indigenous peoples. To get a feel for the difficulty in exploration into the continental inland, we can look at the North American east coast, which arguably was a century ahead of the west coast and California specifically because of its accessibility via the Atlantic Ocean.

At the same time the sixty sheets of Urbano Monte's 1587 map were being published, an English expedition led by John White established the Roanoke Colony on an island off the coast of present-day North Carolina. White, who not only played the role of the colony's governor but also its chief chronicler, decided to return to England later that year to gather much-needed supplies. When he managed to return in 1590, three years after his departure, he was met with a perplexing scene: the entire colony had disappeared. The whereabouts and fate of the Roanoke settlers remain an unresolved mystery, with numerous theories but no definitive answers (Miller, 2000).

Like the cartography we examined regarding San Francisco, John White created a detailed map of Roanoke Island, its surrounding bay, and inland rivers. This map holds significance not only for offering us a window into the past but also because White crafted it amid the distressing backdrop of his return journey, where he found the colony abandoned and sought clues about the whereabouts of its inhabitants, including his daughter and granddaughter (Miller, 2000).

Accompanying the story of Roanoke's disappearance is John White's detailed map, which he crafted during his tenure in the New World. This cartographic document offers a meticulous representation of the region surrounding Roanoke and its neighboring territories (Kuperman, 2011). Beyond being a mere geographical record, the map is a pivotal piece of the puzzle, with specific features that have become the focal point of modern investigations.

John White's cartographic representation of Roanoke Island is a seminal piece in the annals of 16th-century European exploration of North America. Crafted in the late 1580s, White's map demonstrates a methodical approach to cartography, capturing the geographic intricacies of the region with remarkable precision for its epoch.

The map delineates Roanoke Island meticulously, from its rugged coastlines to the adjacent mainland, offering a comprehensive view of the broader Albemarle Sound and its complex estuarine systems. White's inclusion of tidal marshes, barrier islands, and estuarine ecologies indicates an acute observational skill and underscores the area's significance for navigation and potential settlement.

The methodology White likely employed involved a combination of direct observation, rudimentary surveying techniques, and perhaps information gathered from local Native American tribes. Considering the technological constraints of the period, the map stands as a testament to White's dedication to accuracy and the broader English initiative to understand and settle in the New World.

In its entirety, John White's map of Roanoke serves as an invaluable primary source, offering scholars and historians profound insights into the geographic understanding and ambitions of late 16th-century European explorers in North America.

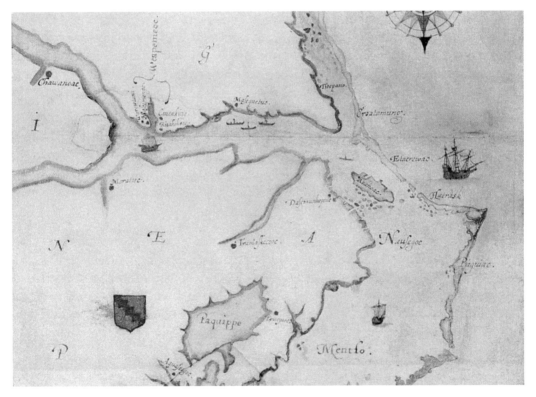

John Whites Map

Primary sources, such as White's map, originate from the time period under study. They are direct, unmediated records or evidence of historical events, often created by witnesses or participants (Turabian, 2018). Examples encompass various materials: manuscripts, letters, diaries, photographs, maps, and even artifacts. These sources are immediate and raw, offering firsthand accounts without later interpretation or alteration (Turabian, 2018).

Conversely, secondary sources interpret, analyze, or draw conclusions from primary sources. They are typically produced after the fact and provide commentary on or discussion of primary source materials (Turabian, 2018). Common examples include history books, articles, and documentaries.

The potency of possessing a primary source, especially one as old as White's map from the late 16th century, cannot be overstated. Given the ravages of time, many such artifacts are lost, deteriorated, or still need to be discovered. When historians access primary documents from such a distant past, they touch the very fabric of the era. It is akin to hearing an unfiltered and genuine voice from centuries ago. This directness provides unparalleled insights, allowing researchers to reconstruct events, understand motivations, and perceive nuances that might be overlooked or misinterpreted by secondary sources.

Thus, the longevity and preservation of White's map provide real value to us today. It is more than a navigational tool; it is a tangible link to the emerging phases of European exploration in North America, offering an undistorted window into that epoch's ambitions, challenges, and perceptions.

It allows us to ask questions directly of its creator. In this case, given the professionalism and urgency of this map and its personal connection to its maker, John White, what would alterations to the map mean? Within the intricate details of White's map, a particular feature warrants rigorous scholarly attention: the distinct patch located at the convergence of the rivers in the interior. This subtle yet deliberate modification raises significant questions: What is under it?

We are not the first to ask this question. This patch became the point of a 2012 study that employed advanced scanning techniques. The aim of the study was not only to understand the patch's compositional characteristics but also to discern any underlying layers or obscured details (British Museum, 2012).

In 2012, experts employed modern scanning techniques to look beneath this patch and uncovered a drawing of a star fort (British Museum, 2012). This revelation has fostered new interpretations and speculations. Today, on this spot is a golf course. The 2012 discovery of the star fort beneath the map's patch has significantly expanded the scope of debates surrounding the Roanoke mystery, potentially connecting it to broader historical and geopolitical contexts.

Given this finding, a reasonable next question is: What is a star fort?

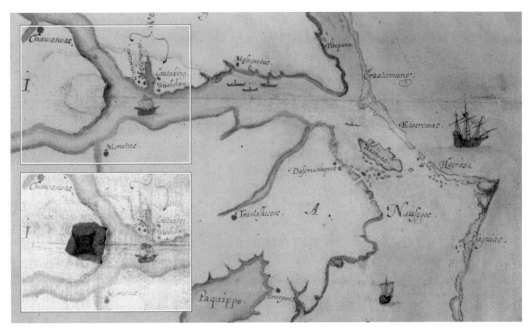

2012 Scan Overlay

2012 British Museum Scan Results Zoom

INTRODUCTION TO STAR FORTS

We are told that star forts, commonly called bastion forts or trace italienne (bastion forts in Italian), represent a pivotal, primarily military, advancement in architecture during the Renaissance. Distinguished by their star-like geometric formations, these structures have been interpreted as strategically designed with protruding bastions to offer comprehensive defensive coverage against invaders (Hale, 1980).

While these fortifications are historically understood to have risen in response to evolving artillery technologies, alternative interpretations about their origins and proliferation have gained traction in certain circles.

Fortification Village of Bourtange

We will soon evaluate the prevailing military theory. Given our ongoing inquiry, it is only prudent to approach the topic of star forts with a healthy dose of skepticism. These forts' uniform design and broad distribution across diverse continents and cultures are thought-provoking. Some argue that this consistency suggests a shared knowledge or technology. The use of this style of building in certain areas poses a challenging question about the dissemination of information. The star's geometry, frequently found in ancient cultures, is often highlighted as a recurring motif with possible deeper meanings.

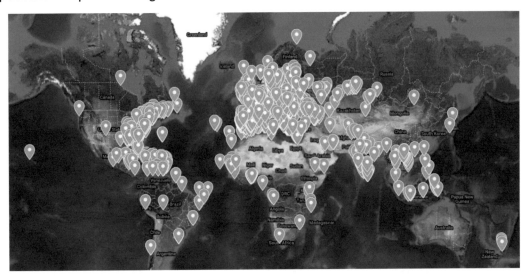

Google Map of Star Forts

Let us examine one of these star forts in North America to see what we can learn about its history.

We are told that following the War of 1812, the U.S. recognized the importance of bolstering its coastal defenses. In 1818, as part of this initiative, the U.S. Army enlisted Benjamin Hopkins of Vermont to construct a substantial masonry fort at Mobile Point, designed by the former military engineer for Napoleon, Simon Bernard. Hopkins succumbed to yellow fever in 1819, having made little progress. Samuel Hawkins, Hopkin's successor, met a similar fate, dying in 1821 without leaving a significant mark on the project (Friend, 2000).

Responsibility then shifted to the United States Army Corps of Engineers under the leadership of Captain René Edward De Russy. Utilizing the hard labor of 200 leased slaves, De Russy and his team painstakingly laid over 30 million cubic yards of high-end red brick.

However, illness forced De Russy to delegate the project to Lieutenant Cornelius Ogden in 1825. By March 1834, Ogden completed the fort's construction, subsequently handing it over to Captain F.S. Belton, commander of Company B, 2nd U.S. Artillery. This unit occupied the fort for approximately 18 months before reassignment to Florida to partake in the Second Seminole War (Friend, 2000).

Fort Morgan, Alabama

The fort's walls, notably integrated with multiple concrete arches, have evolved from the onset of the American Civil War up to the present day. The 200 slaves, we are told, employed the most advanced masonry styles available in the day, a painstaking slow technique typically reserved for well-funded cathedrals and government buildings.

They made the wall over fourteen feet thick, and the arches carry the entire structure's interior, resembling more a Roman Bath than a military fort.

Given the unskilled forced labor, remote location, pressing military need, and logistics of sourcing materials to an almost impossibly inaccessible location, these are odd construction choices, to say the least.

Fort Morgan Interior

It is hard to believe that Fort Morgan's defensive capabilities persistently failed despite its imposing structure and the tremendous labor invested in its construction. As an example of its catastrophes, a significant challenge emerged during the Civil War on August 5, 1864. On this fateful day, the Union fleet, spearheaded by Admiral David Farragut, successfully breached the Confederate defenses at Fort Morgan in the crucial Battle of Mobile Bay. With his renowned rallying cry, "Damn the torpedoes, full speed ahead!" Farragut's forces underscored another moment in Fort Morgan's epic defensive failings (Jones, 2006).

It never held its ground in any siege, consistently capitulating to attacking forces. This stark reality underscores a troubling disparity between its architectural finesse and its glaringly flawed defensive strategy. For all its aesthetic value, it was an abject failure in its primary military role.

The considerable investment of resources, labor, and lives into Fort Morgan starkly contrasts its persistent operational failures. While architecturally, it might represent a high point in red-brick masonry, its performance as a military asset was undeniably lackluster.

WHAT ELSE CAN WE LEARN ABOUT THE HISTORICAL NARRATIVE?

By asking a straightforward question—"Does the commonly accepted origin of San Francisco's name withstand a mild scrutiny of its history?"—we quickly realize that our grasp of history is neither fixed nor absolute. Quite the contrary, the journey through well-established chronicles of American history, as cemented by works such as Lightfoot (2009) and Paddison (1999), uncovers a fascinating anomaly. The San Francisco conundrum, where maps from the 17th and 16th centuries depict the name "San Francisco" long before its name is contemplated and a century before we are told the geography was even discovered, is not just a curious historical quirk. It is a window into more profound, untold stories that lie dormant in historical artifacts and narratives.

The remarkable precision and dedication of cartographers like Guillaume Sanson and Pierre Mariette, combined with the detailed intricacies of Urbano Monte's work, introduce us to a history that challenges our conventional understanding. This departure from the accepted narrative of San Francisco's naming suggests that the city's moniker may have origins far older than we previously believed. This revelation cannot merely be dismissed as an error or speculative labeling, given cartographers' meticulous nature and commitment to accuracy during their times.

Moreover, the discovery of cities depicted on Monte's 1587 map, complete with distinct architectural features, propels our intrigue further. These cities, if temporary settlements or permanent encampments, present a more populated and advanced image of North America than current historical teachings offer.

As we proceed, our objective is to connect the dots between these historical insights and our contemporary understanding. The divergences are unequivocally factual, and it is entirely reasonable for us to investigate them. We must permit ourselves to question prevailing narratives.

The potency of primary sources like these is irrefutable. Such is the case with White's late 16th-century map, a tangible link to the early phases of European exploration in North America. Not just a navigational tool, it offers an undistorted view into the era's ambitions and challenges. It is a map that also begs questions of its own. One such query, pertaining to a mysterious patch at the convergence of rivers in its interior, became the focus of a 2012 study. Employing advanced scanning techniques, experts unearthed an obscure drawing of a star fort beneath the patch, adding a new layer of intrigue to the Roanoke mystery and potentially linking it to broader historical contexts.

The foundations have been set for a deeper dive into the mysteries hidden within these historical gems. As we prepare to embark on subsequent chapters, we will focus on identifying additional historical evidence, leading to an understanding that might push dates in our current timeline around. The objective? To construct a robust, evidence-backed proposal that potentially reshapes our understanding of the historical narrative.

Given that history is fluid and constantly evolving, with previous examples such as the myths surrounding the Great Pyramids and the true discoverers of America, it's reasonable and plausible to suggest that the naming of San Francisco may also harbor a similar untold story. This compelling premise sets the stage for our deeper exploration, seeking answers to the many questions raised and charting a path to rewrite a fragment of our historical tapestry.

We need to research maps and other literary artifacts, get boots on the ground, and explore physical locations and historic structures for new meaning. What are the spires and antennae depicted on these maps? Why are there cities shown that look much more established than our history tells us? Is there a commonality in the architecture of the buildings found at these locations to other buildings in different parts of the world?

The rich world of history can provide promising revelations and insights. We have unearthed just the tip of the iceberg. As we proceed, we aim to uncover more, building a foundation for a proposal that reshapes how we view not just San Francisco's history but North America itself. Join us as we take this incredible journey back in time, challenging the accepted and embracing the mysteries of the past.

Throughout this book, we will endeavor to address the disparities we have uncovered and explore where they may lead. Our focal points will include a deeper dive into San Francisco's history, examining the red markings on ancient maps indicating well-established cities across North America, and an inquiry into the curious depictions of antennas and spires on these maps. We will also delve into primary sources to identify potential alterations similar to those on the John White map, probe the significance of star forts—particularly in North America, where their history raises questions—and finally, cast a wider net across historical narratives to seek further evidence that might illuminate the enigmas we have encountered thus far.

CHAPTER 2: VOYAGES AND VISTAS
THE DRAKE CONTRADICTION

LEWIS & CLARK 1804 - 1806

In the early 19th century, the travels of Meriwether Lewis and William Clark commanded national attention as they embarked on a pioneering expedition that would forever shape American exploration (Ambrose, 1996). From 1804 to 1806, the Lewis and Clark Expedition, authorized by President Thomas Jefferson, bore the monumental objective of unraveling the enigmas concealed within the newly acquired Louisiana Purchase and forging an uncharted course to the Pacific Ocean (Ronda, 1984). Their rigorous journey was paralleled by what we are told is meticulous documentation, painstakenly chronicling geographical landmarks, interactions with indigenous communities, and the cataloging of the rich abundance of natural resources encountered along their route (Lewis & Clark, 2002).

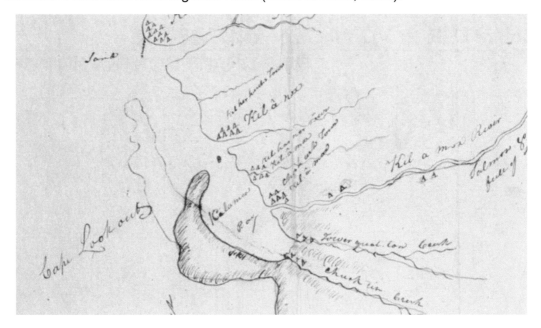

Lewis & Clark Map

Despite the celebrated accomplishments of Lewis and Clark, their cartographic efforts have not entirely escaped critique. Some have regarded their maps as rudimentary compared to other contemporary maps (Edney, 1997). These maps, drawn under the challenging conditions of the expedition and without the benefits of modern technology, were sometimes imprecise and occasionally omitted significant details (Bergon, 1989). This in and of itself is noteworthy, but the idea that Lewis and Clark, in 1806, were somehow dealing with harsher conditions than their Spanish contemporaries from two hundred years prior is a non sequitur.

At this point, anyone can look for themselves and see that the quality of what Lewis and Clark are producing in the way of captured cartography is substantially lower in quality and skill than even John White's map of Roanoke. The John White map is from 1590, which is over two hundred years before Lewis and Clark. With that much time and advancement of technology, we are told that people commissioned by President Jefferson did not possess the ability to create more than rudimentary pencil-based sketches.

It is crucial to recognize the charter underpinning their journey to understand this.

The Lewis and Clark Expedition, often called the Corps of Discovery Expedition (Ronda, 1984), was a direct mandate from President Thomas Jefferson shortly after the Louisiana Purchase. In 1803, the United States made a monumental land deal known as the Louisiana Purchase. For $15 million, the country bought around 828,000 square miles from France, doubling its size (Kukla, 2003).

This land, which spanned from the Mississippi River to the Rocky Mountains and from the Gulf of Mexico up to Canada, had previously been under Spanish and then French control. The French leader, Napoleon Bonaparte, decided to sell due to impending European wars and the challenges of managing such a vast territory (Cerami, 2003).

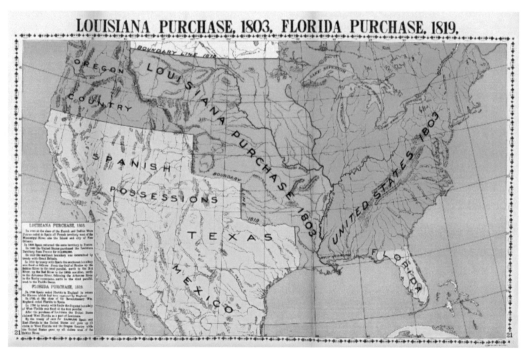

Louisiana Map LOC

President Jefferson initially aimed to buy only a small portion—particularly New Orleans, a key port. However, France's offer of the entire region was too good to pass up. Jefferson faced a constitutional challenge with this purchase, as the U.S. Constitution did not clearly allow for acquiring new land. Nevertheless, seeing the benefits—like trade opportunities, increased security, and room for expansion—he moved forward with the deal (Ellis, 1997).

This purchase was a steppingstone for the U.S., enabling expeditions like Lewis and Clark's and setting the nation on a growth path, leading to 15 new states (Ambrose, 1996).

The Louisiana Purchase is a significant land deal in the history of the United States, and it continues to intrigue many people. France's reasons for selling this large territory are well-documented and mainly linked to geopolitical and financial problems. However, the American desire to acquire this land provides a fascinating context for further exploration.

Historical consensus underscores the importance of New Orleans and its adjacent regions as a strategic port for the flourishing agrarian economy of the U.S. (Kukla, 2003). Thomas Paine, an influential figure of the era, emphasized the importance of the West and the Mississippi River in his writings, suggesting that its control was crucial for American prosperity (Paine, 1802). However, even beyond Paine's assertions, the level of urgency shown by certain American factions raises questions. Could influential figures in American politics and business have hints or subtle indications about the territory's intrinsic value beyond just the river and port control?

Could it be that influential figures in American politics and business had undertaken clandestine surveys or received inside information about the region's potential even before its acquisition? The notable expedition led by Lewis and Clark, which followed the purchase, unveiled the territory's richness. Nevertheless, some U.S. stakeholders' pre-purchase enthusiasm suggests a familiarity beyond mere speculation (Ambrose, 1996).

In the years following the purchase, many individuals and their associates rose to prominence because of this acquisition, securing vast land grants and forging dominant trading routes. The rapidity of expansion into the new territories has led some to speculate about prior knowledge and potential insider connections (Cerami, 2003). Such swift developments echo the urgency of Lewis and Clark's commission to explore the recently acquired land. But the spotlight here is on San Francisco. So, what links these pioneers to this iconic city?

Lewis & Clark Continental Map

Interestingly, even though Lewis and Clark embarked on their exploration three decades after San Francisco was reportedly discovered and named, they never actually traveled south to this specific region. Yet, when referencing the same maps we've examined, they labeled the location on their continental map as "S. Francisco"—the very same designation found on the 1669 Map Amerique Septentrionale."

1669 Map Amerique Septentrionale   *1806 Lewis &Clark*

It's important to note that previous maps have labeled the location we now know as San Francisco as "S. Francisco". Although their accuracy may not match modern maps, it's significant that Lewis and Clark also identified "S. Francisco" in the same area. This alignment between their observations and our current understanding of the region attests to the dependability and accuracy of our findings. We can confidently assert that our discoveries are grounded in historical fact, rather than being a selective interpretation of events to fit a particular narrative.

Additionally, another intriguing detail emerges from the Lewis and Clark map. Positioned directly west of the bay, there is a label denoting the "Port of Sir Frances Drake." This suggests to us a recognition of other historical interactions with the region.

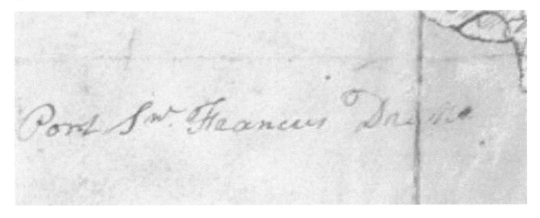

Lewis 7 Clark Map - Port

SIR FRANCIS DRAKE 1580

Sir Francis Drake was a 16th-century English sea captain, navigator, and explorer.

He is best known for circumnavigating the continents from 1577 to 1580, becoming the first English captain to achieve this feat (Kelsey, 1998). In addition to his exploration achievements, Drake played a significant role as a vice admiral in the defeat of the Spanish Armada in 1588. While hailed as a hero in England for his naval successes against the Spanish, the Spanish saw him as a pirate due to his numerous raids on their ships and ports. Drake's voyages expanded English knowledge of the world, paved the way for further English exploration, and established him as one of the most influential navigators in history (Sugden, 1990).

The precise location of Sir Francis Drake's 1579 landing on the California coast remains a subject of academic debate. Historians and researchers have proposed various sites based on analyses of Drake's own descriptions, navigational data, and artifacts found. The most widely accepted theory is that Drake's Cove in Marin County, just north of San Francisco Bay, was the site of the English explorer's encampment, and it was recognized as a National Historic Landmark in 2012. However, other scholars argue for alternative locations, such as Whale Cove farther north or the actual Bay of San Francisco itself. The ambiguity stems from the claimed vagueness of historical records and that Drake's exact routes and stops were not precisely documented (Cummins, 2007).

Here is the exciting thing. This is a modern confusion, and it is unnecessary.

Lewis and Clark were not confused; they listed the Port of Sir Frances Drake on their map. It was/is the Bay of San Francisco. This fact can be dismissed but not ignored; the name Port Sir Frances Drake is physically on the 1806 Lewis and Clark map, labeling the bay next to the label S. Francisco, where San Francisco is today.

However, while the confusion is unnecessary, clarifying the history using real maps created challenged in the current narrative. If you remember in the prior chapter, when we were examining the history of San Francisco, we were told that the bay was missed by all subsequent explorers, including the likes of Juan Rodríguez Cabrillo in 1542 all the way up to Gaspar de Portolà in 1769 who finally found the bay and mapped it.

The question of why San Francisco Bay remained challenging for European explorers to locate raises some skepticism from us in our research regarding the conventional explanations. Modern academics provide all kinds of reasons for this.

Some posit that the narrow entrance to the bay, now marked by the Golden Gate Bridge, could have been overlooked by ships sailing further out to sea, it is worth considering the navigational skills of experienced explorers who often traversed complex waters (Hart, 1978). Similarly, fog in the region, particularly during summer, is mentioned as a factor that might have obscured the bay's entrance. However, the idea that localized weather patterns would deter seasoned mariners could be questioned (Starr, 2007).

San Francisco Bay looking east

Coastal currents and prevailing wind patterns are also suggested as potential hindrances to approaching the shoreline closely enough to discover the bay's entrance. It is essential to consider whether explorers, who were accustomed to navigating diverse and often treacherous waters, would have been deterred by such challenges (Fritscher, 2018).

Another commonly cited explanation revolves around limited exploration along the California coast until the late 18th century. This is attributed to explorers engaging in broader missions or focusing on established harbors to the south, such as Monterey Bay (Rawls & Bean, 2008). However, this perspective prompts us to question whether the navigational expertise of explorers would have been constrained to such an extent that they could not investigate an uncharted coastline more thoroughly.

While indigenous populations like the Ohlone people were aware of and utilized the bay, some argue that limited interaction with European explorers might have hindered the transfer of geographical knowledge. Nevertheless, it could be suggested that explorers would have sought to learn from and communicate with local inhabitants as part of their information-gathering process (Milliken, 1995).

Occam's Razor, our guiding principle favoring more straightforward explanations when faced with multiple hypotheses, sheds light on the origins of the name of San Francisco Bay and its appearance on subsequent maps.

The simplest explanation, supported by historical and cartographical evidence we have provided, suggests that the bay was discovered and named by Sir Francis Drake.

This theory is coherent and aligns with various sources.

If Drake named the location during his 1579 voyage, an original source for the name emerges, harmonizing with known historical facts. This also clarifies the presence of the name on the 1669 Map Amerique Septentrionale and subsequent maps analyzed earlier. While embracing this explanation challenges the established narrative of San Francisco's naming, it offers the most consistent resolution for historiographical inconsistencies.

Historical records indicate that Drake's 1579 voyage along the California coast was characterized by meticulous mapping and documentation of the places he encountered (Kelsey, 1998). The vagueness claims feel contrived to us. As an accomplished explorer and navigator, it is reasonable to assert that he would have recognized and named a significant geographical feature like a bay, especially one as prominent as San Francisco Bay.

Drake's habit of naming landmarks during his voyages is well-documented, exemplified by his naming of "Nova Albion" for present-day California (Kelsey, 1998). It follows that if he had indeed encountered and named San Francisco Bay, this act would have been consistent with his established exploration practices. The subsequent appearance of the bay on later maps could be attributed to the transmission of information through maritime charts, navigation logs, and other sources accessible to cartographers.

The notion that an explorer of Drake's stature, undertaking a voyage of such significance, would not have explored and documented a substantial feature like San Francisco Bay contradicts the principles of prudence. In this case, the simple explanation aligns with the historical context and Drake's exploration practices, making the hypothesis that he discovered and named the bay proper.

This straightforward historical clarification raises additional inquiries.

What specific geographic aspects of the bay motivated Drake to designate it as San Francisco?

Why did historians previously encounter difficulties in preserving the coherence of its naming history?

Are there beneficiaries of this altered historical narrative?

Does obfuscating the real history serve to confuse certain aspects intentionally or perhaps alludes to alternative notions?

The names S. Francisco and San Francisco are clearly in use before our given history of 1775/6.

We have a reference to Sir Frances Drake, an actual historical figure who landed in the area and had a habit of naming locations. Soon after his voyage, the name San Francisco started appearing on maps. There is no compelling historical data that we could find in our exhaustive research that expressly excluded Drake as the true discoverer of San Francisco Bay; he is just ignored.

He has been omitted from the narrative.

We will come back to this mystery in a few pages. Let's focus on what else was happening in North America as it was being established.

CHAPTER 3: THIRD SYSTEM DESIGN
OVER-ENGINEERED GLORIOUS FAILURES

FORT POINT, SAN FRANCISCO

Our inquiry started with a simple question about the historical narrative for the name of San Francisco. The investigation took us to old maps, which also exposed an oddity across the North American continent during this early time period. We discovered that at the same time Sir Frances Drake was sailing around the oceans, mapping all the continents, a star fort was hidden on the 1587 John White map. Our intention was not necessarily a transcontinental linkage to disparate mysteries, but it is what we found and where we ended up.

When conducting this type of research, there is an element of allowing the data to take you wherever it leads. This is precisely the essence of syntopical analysis, an approach articulated by the 1940s philosopher and educator Morton J. Adler. Adler's Syntopical Analysis method embraces the intricate web of historical documents to unearth the subtle connections that transcend time and context.

Adler's approach employs a methodology that translates historical books, maps, literature, and other artifacts into ideas, where key terms and concepts are identified, collated, and compared. This process enables a panoramic examination of the evolving ideas that traverse various documents, shedding light on how they interact, shape, and diverge over time. This is the methodology we are employing here in this book. By tracing these conceptual trajectories, syntopical analysis uncovers the shared themes, divergent viewpoints, and points of convergence that define the evolving narrative of human intellect. It is an approach that traverses the expanses of historical discourse, illuminating the diverse tapestry of ideas woven across different eras and historical contexts (Adler, 1940).

To stay true to this methodology, we have to ask the question. If star forts were found hidden on a map from the same time period with all of the inconsistencies concerning the naming of San Francisco, were star forts also present in San Francisco? If so, do their histories survive the same level of superficial scrutiny that caused the naming of San Francisco to collapse under its own weight?

We conducted more research and yes, it turns out there are star forts in San Francisco with impractical historical narratives. One fort, called Fort Point, is currently preserved under the Golden Gate Bridge. A second fort was said to have been built on Alcatraz Island in the same style as Fort Point, something called the Third System. We will cover the Third System design in a moment. That said, while Fort Alcatraz is designated as a Third System fort, we do not find that to be the case under close examination. Here, we will treat Fort Point as the only Third System structure on the west coast. After we analyze Fort Point and delve into Third System structures, we will return to Alcatraz to explain our reasoning once everything has been laid out.

As we turn our attention to the Fort Point star fort, we find ourselves on the precipice of the 1850s—a time of transformation in San Francisco. The city, which in the 1830s was a humble settlement of something between 200 and 1,000 people (the numbers are fuzzy, but nowhere is it any many more people than this that we could find), underwent a metamorphosis of epic proportions within a mere decade. By the close of the 1840s, the Gold Rush had transformed this modest settlement into a lively hub, its population growing from very few people in 1846 to a modest 25,000 by 1850 (Issel & Cherny, 1986). Nevertheless, as the city did adapt to the growing population, questions arise about its capacity to embark on monumental construction projects like Fort Point between 1853 and 1861.

Fort Point with Golden Gate Bridge built over top of it, 1960s

For one, the sudden influx of people, while an advantage in numbers, brought challenges in skilled labor availability. The population consisted mainly of gold prospectors—not trained masons or military architects. The expertise required to construct a defense structure of Fort Point's caliber would have been specialized, calling into question the city's readiness for such an undertaking (Weaver, 2001). This is also the city's boom period, so remember that where they may have been skilled masons, they could earn a much better living being paid top dollar to build out the rest of the city compared to a low-wage government contract in the dangerous conditions of the time.

Material acquisition poses another puzzle. Narratives hint at granite imported from China to lay Fort Point's foundation (Golden et al., 2023). However, why would a city in a country with granite quarries opt for such a far-fetched and costly procurement method? Similarly, while the vicinity boasted brick-making capabilities, the scale and quality required for a project like Fort Point would likely have been a stretch (Weaver, 2001).

If the construction of this fort were as urgent as we are told with anticipation of the coming war, the delays and logistics of sourcing materials from the other side of the world would seem incongruent. Transportation, a crucial cog in the construction machinery, was still budding in San Francisco. Despite the port's vibrancy, thanks to the Gold Rush, the city's internal transportation networks were not as mature. This begs the question: How feasible was moving massive quantities of materials and a workforce across the city from the docks?

Fort Point Interior

To add some perspective, in 1853, when the Fort Point project started, the U.S. military's decision to procure substantial quantities of granite from China was fraught with diplomatic and logistical challenges. It is near impossible for us to understand how military leadership of any confidence level could land on this plan. At this time, official diplomatic ties between the U.S. and China were nascent. Although the Treaty of Wanghia had been signed in 1844, establishing some foundational trade relationships (Fairbank, 1969), the level of diplomatic engagement was still rudimentary.

The U.S. had not yet established a permanent ambassadorial post in China by 1853. Instead, the nation relied on consular representation in key trading ports, notably Canton (modern-day Guangzhou) (Spence, 1999). While these consuls were instrumental in fostering trade and safeguarding American interests, their capacity was limited, given the vastness of China and the intricate complexities of its regional politics and trade dynamics.

Fort Point Interior 2

Furthermore, considering the expansive domestic sources of granite available within the U.S., the decision to import from a distant and diplomatically unfamiliar territory (LaFeber, 1997) suggests to us brazen incompetence. The U.S., particularly in regions close to San Francisco, had ample granite reserves, which could have ensured a more reliable, timely, and cost-effective supply for the military project. Utilizing domestic sources would have also eliminated potential challenges associated with long maritime journeys, customs, tariffs, and the unpredictability of international trade during that era (Pomeranz & Topik, 2006).

Given the low state of diplomatic relations and high state of domestic alternatives, the U.S. military's choice to source granite from China in 1853 appears to have been impractical at its most gracious. If the charter and urgency for coastal fortifications in preparation for an impending civil war were driving decisions, then we are dealing with an impossibly poor set of military leaders. As we look into the mysterious Third System strategy, the decision to source foundational materials from China completely collapses as an impossibility.

Furthermore, it's bewildering that the decision mentioned earlier was made without considering the fact that the city's economy and infrastructure largely relies on gold prospecting and related industries. Was there even enough economic infrastructure in place to support a massive construction project sourced from foreign countries? Adding to the complexity, the city was undergoing rapid changes, and its governance and security structures were still evolving. These structures are crucial for a project of this magnitude (Rawls & Orsi, 1999).

At the heart of this enigma is the transportation landscape of the mid-19th century, never mind the social-political mess of a foreign relationship that was already debilitating. The era's maritime capabilities were not designed for transporting vast quantities of dense cargo like granite over thousands of miles of unpredictable ocean (Gibbins, 2001).

Every shipping endeavor during this era came with its fair share of risks. The frequency of shipwrecks during the period is a testament to the perilous nature of oceanic transport (Gibbins, 2001). Each shipment of granite would not only have to contend with these maritime dangers but would also require a tremendous amount of time, potentially slowing down the construction process substantially while simultaneously occupying time on the docks built for the gold trade.

Then comes the consideration of ship capacity. With the limited carrying ability of ships in the 19th century, one must question how many voyages, ships, or even fleets of ships, were needed to transport the sheer volume of granite required for Fort Point's robust foundation. The mind boggles at such an endeavor's logistical planning, time, and financial cost.

We can do some simple math to frame the immense job it would have been to ship enough granite from China. The fort's walls are roughly 250 feet long. If we assume a foundation requirement of ten feet wide and fifteen feet deep (generally modest for supporting the eight million bricks of the structure), we end up with 165,000 cubic feet of foundational material; in this case, history tells us granite.

Granite weighs roughly 168 pounds per cubic foot (U.S. Geological Survey, various years). This means the foundation in granite for Fort Point would weigh roughly 27,720,000 pounds or 13,860 tons. Historical records suggest that the carrying capacity of mid-19th-century ships varied, but practical considerations meant they were not always loaded to their total tonnage. One such type of vessel that might have been used in a means of transport like this might be a "barque" or "bark," a sailing ship with three or more masts. Another type could be "brigantines" or "brigs". These ships were more common for carrying heavy cargo over long distances. (Chapelle, 1935).

While capacity and tonnage varied wildly, a mid-sized transport ship of the era built for heavy cargo would reasonably be built to transport 500 tons. We will use 80% capacity, given that these crews were not on suicide runs and would not have sailed this distance overloaded. This provides the following math:

- Practical Load per Ship = 0.80 x 500 tons = 400 tons/ship
- Number of Ships Needed = 13,860 tons ÷ 400 tons/ship = 35 ships

These logistics seem infeasible when we have the availability of resources closer to home. For example, the Raymond Granite Quarry, located in Raymond California, is only 150 miles away from the Fort Point construction site. There were also quarries present in the southeastern Atlantic states (Dale, 1910).

There is also the Raymond Granite Quarry, located in Raymond, California, which is only 150 miles away from the Fort Point construction site.

Nevertheless, we are told that the decision to import granite from China made more sense for a military project that was to become the strategic key to the entire west coast. Since these domestic resources were accessible, it raises questions about why builders would opt for a distant and complicated overseas source. This becomes even more perplexing when considering the rapid growth of San Francisco during the Gold Rush era. The city's port was bustling with activity, mostly centered around the influx of hopeful gold seekers and transporting gold (Rawls & Orsi, 1999). Amidst this frenzy, diverting resources and focusing on facilitating massive granite imports appears unconventional.

The narrative surrounding Fort Point's granite foundation pushed us to reflect on the larger context of 19th-century construction, transportation, and decision-making. While the fort might be a testament to architectural elegance, the sourcing choices made during its construction remain enigmatic and warrant deep skepticism.

We will need to unravel all of this. Using Occam's Razor, our initial analysis here suggests two things. The foundation was not imported Chinese granite. It is logistically impossible. If local quarries were also not used (as history tells us), what possible conclusion about constructing the fort's foundation can we reach?

Let us briefly table the logistics concerning materials and examine the other side of the equation, labor. Who will be building this granite foundation and doing the detailed mason work?

THE GOLD MINERS' CONUNDRUM: FROM PANS TO MASONRY

Fort Point's construction story continues to become more convoluted. We are told that gold miners, previously absorbed in the frenzied quest for riches in the Californian terrain, suddenly transformed into builders of an architectural marvel. Mining, as described in the annals of the Gold Rush, demanded persistence, physical endurance, and at times, a degree of fortune (Rawls & Orsi, 1999). Nevertheless, none of these qualities naturally translate into the finesse and precision required for sophisticated masonry.

Fort Morgan Interior (Third System Masonry)

Masonry, particularly of the standard exhibited at Fort Point, is a complex craft demanding years of training. It is not merely about placing bricks but about understanding the intricacies of materials, architectural design, and engineering principles. Can one genuinely believe that individuals more accustomed to the dirt and grit of mines could seamlessly transition into master craftsmen within a short span?

The commendation of Fort Point's masonry is undeniable. References to its "solid masonry of more than ordinary artistic skill" (Weaver, 2001) place the fort's construction not merely as a functional endeavor but as a work of art. Such high praise is typically reserved for the handiwork of experienced artisans. However, can such excellence be attributed to miners whose previous endeavors were hardly related to building, let alone artistic masonry?

The narrative's underpinnings lean heavily on a tale of transformation – miners redirecting their dreams from gold to bricks. Does this narrative account for the nuances of skill acquisition, especially in a field as demanding as masonry? Eight years, while substantial, could be argued as insufficient for a complete novice to attain mastery, especially when crafting something as intricate as Fort Point. Further compressing the timetable is that the miners first must have shifted their expertise to granite foundations, a deep skill of its own, then again made a second transition to become the pinnacle of masonry superiority.

Fort Pulaski Interior (Third System Masonry)

As per the narrative, the miners' sudden skill pivot raises eyebrows. It opens a realm of questions that the available documentation does not satisfactorily address. The narrative's gaps prompt skepticism. Piecing together the true story necessitates addressing these questions head-on, especially when anomalies starkly contrast the accepted tale.

AGAINST THE CLOCK: THE CHALLENGE OF THE EIGHT-YEAR TIMELINE

A construction project's foundation determines the structure's strength and longevity. This is particularly true for monumental buildings like Fort Point. Therefore, it is crucial to appreciate the inherent time requirements of laying down a robust foundation when analyzing the construction timeline. With Fort Point's foundation reportedly made of granite shipped from afar (Weaver, 2001), the initial logistical hurdles multiply.

Firstly, one must question the actual time taken to procure the granite. 19th-century shipping was unpredictable: changing weather, ship malfunctions, and lengthy sea routes across a thirty-something-ship armada traversing the Pacific Ocean, each laden to its near limit. Just the time taken for a single shipment to be loaded, travel from China, be unloaded, and be processed for construction could span months (Gibbins, 2001). This timeframe extends further if multiple shipments were involved, which is likely given the granite volume needed for such a colossal project, as we have demonstrated.

Once the granite arrived, the actual foundational work began. Here, it is essential to acknowledge that foundational work is not just about laying down stones. It requires leveling the ground, ensuring stability, fitting the stones in place, and guaranteeing that they can bear the weight of the massive brick structure that would be built on top. In the 19th century, without the aid of modern machinery and technologies, this was labor-intensive and demanded a significant amount of time (Dale, 1910). A conservative estimate of 2 to 3 years solely for foundational work seems plausible. However, this raises a critical concern about the remaining timeline. This timeline is also generous; it would not be unreasonable for the fort's location on a rocky peninsula jutting out as the breakwater between the Pacific Ocean and San Francisco Bay could present additional logistical challenges, further extending the foundation work timeline.

Subtracting foundational years from the eight-year timeline leaves a mere 5 to 6 years for the entire superstructure. The math becomes increasingly dubious considering it is stated that eight million bricks were used. Out of the 200 converted gold miners we are told built the fort; each worker would be responsible for laying approximately 650 bricks daily for six consecutive years. This staggering statistic does not factor in days lost to inclement weather, injuries, or other unforeseen halts in construction (Rawls & Orsi, 1999).

However, the narrative does not just present a fort built swiftly; it describes a fort of extraordinary masonry quality. The expertise required to precisely lay bricks, ensuring the walls are straight, even, and capable of withstanding attacks, is not insignificant. For such skilled work, the rate of bricklaying would inevitably decrease. Further, we can see today that the choice of masonry style was the most advanced, time-consuming, and difficult possible.

To cover the basics for understanding, in the realm of masonry, the way in which bricks are laid dictates not only the visual aesthetic of a wall but also its structural integrity. Three foundational brick-laying patterns, or bonds, commonly appear in various architectural works.

The simplest among these is the **Stretcher Bond**, often called the Running Bond. Here, bricks are placed in linear sequences, each offset by half a brick from its neighboring row. Due to its straightforward methodology, entry-level masons frequently utilize this bond (Ching & Adams, 2001).

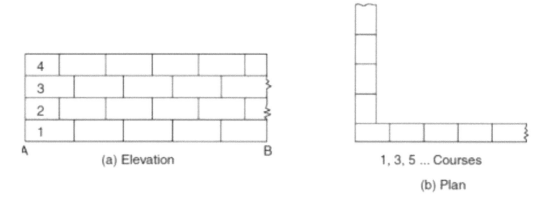

(a) Elevation

1, 3, 5 ... Courses

(b) Plan

Stretcher Bond

A more intricate bond, the **English Bond**, an intermediate masonry skill, alternates entire courses of headers and stretchers. This style requires meticulous attention to ensure that bricks in consecutive rows do not align their vertical joints, subsequently enhancing the wall's stability (McCarthy, 2005).

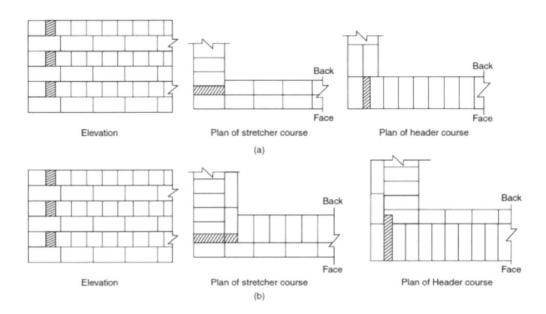

Elevation   Plan of stretcher course   Plan of header course

(a)

Elevation   Plan of stretcher course   Plan of Header course

(b)

English Bond

Perhaps the most sophisticated of the three, the **Flemish Bond**, artfully combines headers and stretchers within the same course. This results in a rhythmic pattern, which demands precise alignment for each brick, creating an interplay of aesthetics and robustness in construction. Any misplacement can easily disrupt the bond's uniformity, reflecting the complexity of its execution (Hodgson, 1906).

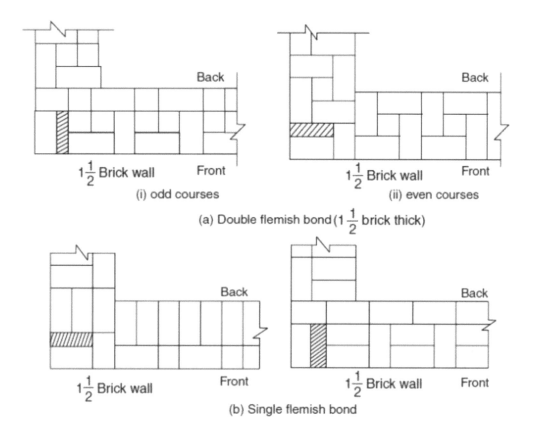

Flemish Bond

The choice of a bond often stems from a confluence of design aspirations, structural requirements, and the mason's expertise. As you may expect by now, on top of the other logistical challenges in the construction of Fort Point, the masonry style used is primarily Flemish Bond. It is challenging to see how novice masons could achieve both the speed and the quality the narrative suggests. Furthermore, the fort's design, inspired by the "Third System," is intricate, requiring even more time for details like casemates (complex structural interior arches) and other advanced architectural features (Weaver, 2001).

When analyzing the combined intricacies of foundational work, brick masonry, and design intricacies within an eight-year window, the narrative becomes not just ambitious but ventures into the realm of implausibility. The pressures of such a tight timeline would challenge not only the quality of the work but also the physical and mental well-being of the workers involved. This discrepancy further underscores the necessity for a more rigorous examination of the narrative's authenticity.

Remember, we have been told all these bizarre decisions to make building the Fort Point fortification as logistically difficult as possible were made by a group of senate-appointed senior military leaders whose charter was to maximize US assets in preparation for the looming Civil War. We will chronicle that military body as we try and understand what this Third System strategy truly was.

THIRD SYSTEM DESIGN: THE WEST COAST ANOMALY

When examining the fortifications that dot the landscape of America's coasts, one finds a pattern of strategic defense principles that were developed and refined over time. The Third System of coastal defense, formulated in the aftermath of the War of 1812, stands as a testament to the military architectural innovation of its era - or so we are meant to believe. With its dense fortifications predominantly focused on the Eastern Seaboard, its presence in San Francisco's Fort Point appears as an outlier (Weaver, 2001).

During the 19th century, the West Coast was not facing the same maritime threats as the East. The Eastern Seaboard, with its historical engagements, especially with European powers, had tangible reasons to develop and adopt advanced defense mechanisms. The strategic decision to apply the Third System — with its renowned layered defense, formidable masonry walls, and multi-tiered gun positions — was a direct reaction to the vulnerabilities the East Coast experienced during the War of 1812. So, the natural question arises: Why transplant this specific design to a geographically and strategically different coast?

The Pacific Coast, primarily during the early to mid-19th century, had different geopolitical and security considerations. Threats from the Pacific were not as immediate or pronounced as those from the Atlantic. Arguably, the rapid socio-economic shifts in San Francisco, especially post-Gold Rush, brought the harbor and its assets into sharp focus, meriting more robust defenses (Rawls & Orsi, 1999). However, even accepting the need for a fort, why choose the Third System, an expensive, labor-intensive design, for Fort Point? Moreover, as we have chronicled already, why also choose the most complex logistical methods and masonry strategies?

One might argue that an element of prestige is associated with the Third System. This seems to be what we are supposed to imply from the history as offered. However, prestige guided by a one-size-fits-all approach, given the real threats of the time period, makes little sense. Also, in hindsight, while the narrative is that these fortifications were commissioned with knowledge of "the impending civil war," we suggest that independent, authoritative accounts of 1853 West Coast America cannot really claim this. While there is ample evidence that tensions were high in 1853, and many recognized the divisive nature of the issues at hand, the idea of a catastrophic civil war tearing the nation apart in the near future might not have been universally acknowledged or believed (McPherson, 1988).

In its most generous spotlight, using such a design could have been seen as a way of bolstering the reputation of San Francisco as a city of prominence. Nevertheless, this introduces another inconsistency. If the goal was to showcase might and grandeur, then the exclusive use of the Third System for just one fort and nowhere else along the California Coast is puzzling. An endeavor so significant would typically have a well-documented rationale, yet the narrative surrounding Fort Point's design choice remains veiled in ambiguity.

Furthermore, constructing such a fort requires resources and specialized expertise. The intricacies of the Third System design are not novice friendly. Given the earlier discussions on the workforce comprised of erstwhile gold miners, the question of how such a complex design was executed with precision becomes even more pressing. A near-infinite set of alternative fort designs or defensive strategies could have been used at a fraction of the cost and time and near the same effectiveness levels.

In essence, Fort Point stands as a West Coast anomaly. While the city's economic and strategic importance in the 19th century is undeniable, the decision to exclusively implement the Third System design at this location and not elsewhere on the Pacific Coast seems incongruous. Without clear, corroborated documentation, this aspect of the fort's history continues to challenge historical interpretations and begs more in-depth exploration.

We will do a deep dive into this Third System design in a moment, but first, let us clear up the rest of the Fort Point historical record.

REASSESSING THE HISTORICAL RECORD OF FORT POINT

Historical accounts offer invaluable insights into our past, painting a vivid image of past epochs. However, they can occasionally present information that, when closely scrutinized, raises more questions than it answers. The narrative surrounding Fort Point's construction proves to be a classic case in point.

The decision to use granite imported from China, thousands of miles across the vast Pacific, during the mid-19th century is baffling. Shipping technology and logistics of the era were not particularly advanced (Gibbins, 2001). The vast amount of granite required for the foundation would necessitate multiple voyages, each fraught with potential dangers, including shipwrecks, piracy, and unfavorable weather conditions. The logical, economical, and timely choice would have been to source materials locally or from nearby regions that are well-documented to have existed.

Another intriguing element is the purported transformation of gold miners into masons. Gold mining, as a skill, is worlds apart from the exacting science and art of masonry (Rawls & Orsi, 1999). The claim that these miners, perhaps disheartened by their failed gold endeavors, suddenly transformed into master Flemish Bond bricklayers constructing "solid masonry of more than ordinary artistic skill" is perplexing. Gold mining required endurance and grit, whereas masonry demanded precision, an understanding of materials, and specific skills. Would it not have been more feasible to employ individuals with prior masonry experience, especially for such an ambitious project?

The construction timeline further complicates matters. Establishing a solid foundation, particularly for a mammoth structure like Fort Point, is no small feat. If one assumes that laying the foundation alone took 2-3 years (given the granite's import), this leaves a mere 5-6 years for the remainder of the construction. The eight million bricks reportedly used in the fort's construction pose yet another challenge. If calculated, this would mean a staggering number of bricks laid each day by every worker. Achieving both quantity and the reported quality in such a tight timeframe would be a Herculean task, to say the least.

Lastly, the narrative underscores Fort Point as the sole Third System fort on the California Coast (Weaver, 2001). Fort Alcatraz, which we will discuss later, was built near the same time, and was classified as a Third System fort even though it was not one.   This leaves Fort Point's implementation in the area as very puzzling. If this design was superior, offering better defensive capabilities, why was it not widely adopted across the Pacific Coast? Was Fort Point an experimental endeavor? Given the history and tensions of the time, was this the place for such experimentation?

In totality, when we piece together these aspects, the construction narrative of Fort Point appears fraught with inconsistencies. It beckons historians, researchers, and readers alike to probe deeper, question the accepted, and continually seek corroborative evidence.

Such anomalies in historical narratives emphasize the importance of rigorous academic inquiry. They serve as timely reminders that while the past might be built in brick and stone, our understanding of it is not. Moreover, as stewards of history, we are responsible for sifting through these accounts with a discerning eye, always pursuing the actual truth over the presented narrative.

THIRD SYSTEM FORTIFICATIONS: ANALYSIS

We need to build an understanding of this Third System as it is used as the justification for the over-engineering of Fort Point. It is also used as the over-engineering excuse for several other star forts of the time. We will examine them as we investigate this Third System design.

Third System Design – Form over Function

We are told that in the wake of the War of 1812, America faced an unsettling revelation – its coastal fortifications were glaringly inadequate. While the U.S. had managed to endure the conflict with its sovereignty intact, encounters with British naval forces highlighted significant vulnerabilities in the nation's coastal defense (Smith, 1992). Recognizing this, the U.S. embarked on an audacious coastal defense overhaul, termed the "Third System."

Unlike its predecessors, the Third System was both expensive and elaborate. The design was marked by masonry walls, built to withstand not just the direct assault of enemy infantry but also the increasingly destructive power of naval artillery. These fortifications also featured tiered casemates, and multi-level enclosures that housed artillery, thereby maximizing firepower and protecting the gun crews (Lewis, 2001).

However, questions arise when we consider the uniformity and consistency of these design features. Why, for instance, did some forts possess more tiered casemates than others? Was it solely based on the expected threat level, or were there other factors, like budgetary constraints or logistical challenges, at play? We get very few details about *HOW* this Third System's design decisions were made. We are told the need, but walking a military strategy from the need to improved coastal defenses to sinking massive time and resources into building overly complex architectural marvels seems a strange output from a group of practical military minds still reeling from the War of 1812.

The Third System design, we are told, was the brainchild of the Board of Engineers for Fortifications, with key figures like Joseph G. Totten driving the design and strategy (Harrison, 2008). Joseph G. Totten's role during the War of 1812 certainly offers cause for reflection. After graduating from the U.S. Military Academy at West Point in 1805, Totten took on the role of an engineer during this conflict, directly engaging in constructing and defending several fortifications. Unfortunately, the war was marked by significant defensive failings on the American side. Despite facing these fortifications, British forces succeeded in capturing and burning parts of Washington, D.C., highlighting glaring inadequacies in the country's defensive strategy (Hickey, 1989).

Fort Jefferson (Third System Architecture)

Given the shortcomings that were so clearly exposed during the War of 1812, it is perplexing that Totten, who was involved in these flawed defenses, would later ascend to a leadership role overseeing the revamp of American coastal defenses. By 1838, he was Chief of the U.S. Army Corps of Engineers. One has to question: Was Totten's promotion a result of genuine merit or a consequence of strategic maneuvering within military circles? His rapid progression, especially after such evident failures in the war, casts a shadow on the decision-making process of the time. Did the military leadership truly believe Totten was the solution or were other dynamics at play? It is difficult to reconcile the trust placed in him with the evident failures of the fortifications he was previously involved with (Mahon, 1972).

The utter and complete failing of this Third System reinforces our skepticism.

Forts of the Third System prominently dotted the Eastern and Gulf Coasts. However, their representation on the West Coast was surprisingly absent, with Fort Point being a notable exception. One must question why such a design was used at all (Weaver, 2001). Was it to counter a perceived threat not clearly identified in the historical narratives? To deal with logistical hurdles? Or, perhaps, as a bias in strategic thinking towards the Eastern Seaboard?

While the Third System forts' structural integrity and strategic placement were commendable, their performance during the Civil War gave rise to skepticism. Despite its impressive construction, Fort Sumter, another example of Third System design, fell after prolonged bombardment, signaling the changing dynamics of warfare (Martin, 1995). Did the engineers and strategists behind these fortifications overestimate their resilience or underestimate the technological advancements in artillery?

Or, as history shows us, were these Third System forts not at all designed for the warfare of their time?

Fort Sumter's Humbling

Fort Sumter's surrender, following the extended bombardment from Confederate forces, remains one of the most prominent examples of the Third System's vulnerabilities. Strategically located at Charleston Harbor, South Carolina, its masonry walls were designed to resist long assaults. Nevertheless, it fell and was captured multiple times during the war (Martin, 1995). This episode raises concerns about whether these forts' designs effectively matched warfare's realities.

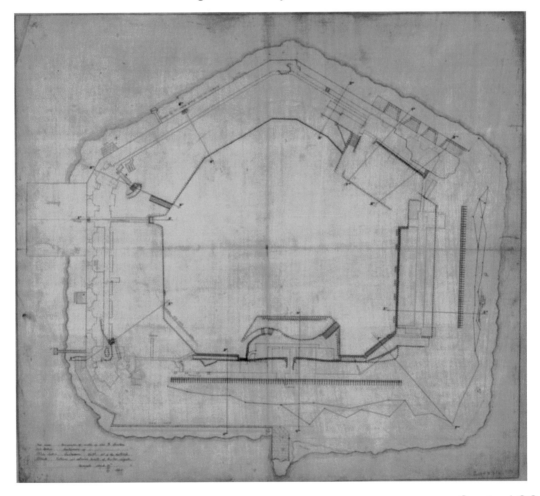

Sumter LOC

THE FUTILITY OF FORT MORGAN

Another emblematic case was Fort Morgan at the entrance of Mobile Bay, Alabama. Despite its thick walls and strategic position, Fort Morgan consistently capitulated under pressure. The fort's repeated falls shadowed the Third System's lack of true capabilities, making one wonder if there were inherent strategic flaws (Harris, 2007).

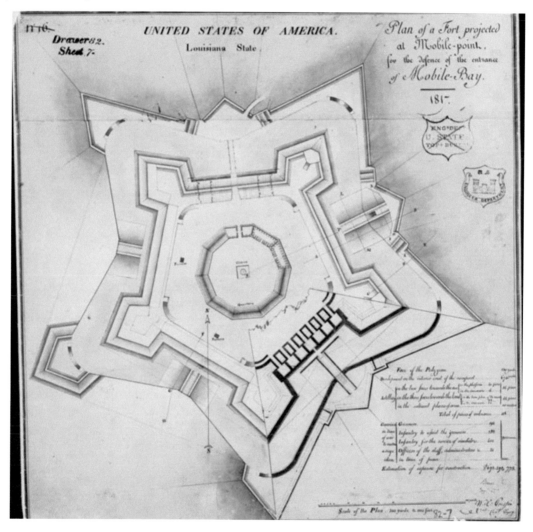

Fort Morgan LOC

FORT PULASKI'S BREACH

On the coast of Georgia, Fort Pulaski was deemed invincible with walls of 7.5 feet thick. However, during the Civil War, Union forces, using rifled artillery, breached the walls and forced a surrender after a mere 30 hours of bombardment (Castel, 1993). This incident underscored the glaring mismatch between the fort's design and the evolving warfare technologies.

Pulaski 1924

FORT GAINES' QUICK CAPITULATION

Located opposite Fort Morgan at the entrance to Mobile Bay, Fort Gaines similarly met a fate of military disappointment. Despite its substantial defensive design, it surrendered quickly during the Battle of Mobile Bay, unable to provide a sustained defense (Harris, 2007).

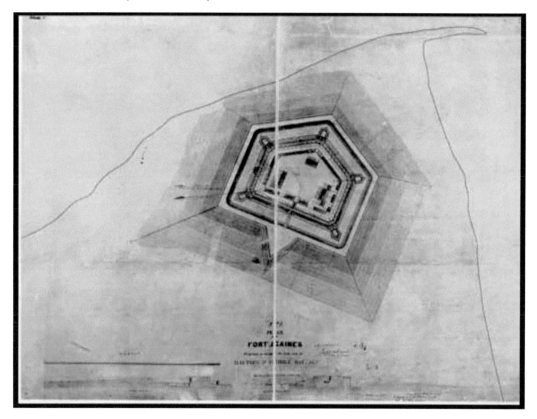

Gaines

FORT MACON'S INSUFFICIENCIES

Fort Macon was believed to be a stronghold in North Carolina. However, its defenses were quickly compromised when besieged by Union forces in 1862, leading to its capture (Barrett, 1963). Such a swift fall prompts questions about the effectiveness of the defensive strategies employed in these structures.

Macon NC

To tie off our analysis of Fort Alcatraz, many of its construction's historical details and records are missing from the archives. Fort Alcatraz is a unique deviation from the standardized designs of the Third System coastal fortifications (Weaver, 2001). Its architectural layout is immediately distinct, breaking away from the typical geometric shapes with tiered casemates as seen in Third System forts. When it comes to armaments, Fort Alcatraz diverges again. Fort Alcatraz exhibits an alternative configuration rather than featuring the usual multiple tiers of gun casemates and an open barbette tier (Manucy, 1985).

Furthermore, in terms of sheer size, Fort Alcatraz's footprint is notably smaller than Third System fortifications that dot the Atlantic coast. One standout feature is the fort's barracks: in a departure from the norm, the barracks on Alcatraz were not enclosed or covered in the manner seen in many Third System designs. Lastly, much, if not all, of the original construction work has been obscured over time in the location's transformation from fort to prison. Little remains of the complex Flemish Bond masonry style in any academic studies we could find in our extensive research.

Despite its visionary approach, the Third System is riddled with ambiguities and inconsistencies. Its selective implementation across coasts, the potential influences from European designs, and varying combat performance demand a more critical examination. History, in its essence, is a tapestry of facts, interpretations, and, sometimes, oversights. Our exploration into the Third System reminds us of this intricate weave.

The recurring failures of the Third System fortifications during their pivotal tests in the Civil War era are unmistakable. They were consistently outmatched by superior enemy strategy, evolving artillery technology, or perhaps due to inherent design flaws. These shortcomings emphasize the peril of not adapting military designs to the rapidly changing landscapes of warfare.

While the Third System fortifications were undeniably architectural marvels of their era, their military efficacy during combat scenarios was underwhelming. Their repeated failures in the face of enemy assaults accentuate the gap between their anticipated and actual combat performance. This serves as a cautionary tale, underscoring the importance of aligning military designs with the practicalities of warfare.

CHAPTER 4: THE GREAT FIRES 1849 TO 1851

THAT TIME SAN FRANCISCO BURNED DOWN SIX TIMES IN A YEAR AND A HALF

GOOD THINGS APPARENTLY KEEP ON BURNING

The strategic choices behind the construction of Fort Point are baffling.

Given the constraints of early 1850s San Francisco, the decisions to use specific materials and construction methods, seemingly advanced for their time and notably advanced for this region (Bancroft, 1888), raise questions.

We must dig deeper into the context of the times; was San Francisco during the early 1850s without challenges? What were the prevailing conditions and circumstances influencing the military's decision-making for Fort Point's construction? While substantive evidence may exist to support these choices, we could not find it, and a closer examination of the historical context just raises further questions about the rationale behind such decisions.

In 1846, when the U.S. government acquired Alcatraz Island for purported military purposes, the motivations behind this acquisition were not entirely clear (Eldredge, 1912). The eventual significance of this acquisition would only be realized with the California Gold Rush in 1848, a monumental event that was yet to unfold (Brands, 2002). It prompts the question: Was the government's foresight exceptionally prescient, or was the purchase driven by other, perhaps unrecorded, factors? Purchasing Alcatraz Island was a brilliant military move, but it was done before the event that made it brilliant happened. Just like the naming of San Francisco, which we discovered earlier, in the same way, the military history here is out of sequence for some reason.

To set the context, San Francisco was a relatively quiet settlement before the rush of settlers eager to stake their claim during the Gold Rush (Holliday, 1999). The population was sparse, and the sudden influx post-1848 would have rapidly escalated demands on infrastructure. We will review a few of the buildings built during this period that would have been competing for resources with Fort Point. However, there are too many structures to review all of them. As will become apparent as we chronicle the devastations, potentially four to eight thousand San Francisco buildings were built, destroyed, rebuilt, destroyed, rebuild, destroyed, and so on.

We are told that the early buildings were hastily constructed using timber (Dillon, 1961). One must consider the origins of these building materials. The original structures would have sourced local materials, but those materials were quickly exhausted. Given the pace of construction and consecutive rebuilds after a long run of disasters, it is a matter of logistical and economic curiosity about where these additional construction resources were sourced (Issel & Cherny, 1986). The narrative, interestingly, forces linkage in materials from Europe and Asia, but the sheer volume of materials, as we will review, almost certainly makes their acquisition impossible, no matter the sources.

We are told that wooden structures, closely packed, became a characteristic feature of San Francisco during this time (Bean, 1952). While this might have been a short-term solution to accommodate the rapidly increasing population, it provides an excuse for the First Great Fire. The first of six, between 1849 and 1851, San Francisco experienced a series of fires that decimated its growing urban landscape (Richards, 1987). What is striking is the city's resilience and its ability to rebuild after each calamity; when you look at the early history, we are told the town was rebuilt from the ground up a half-dozen or more times within the first hundred or so years of its founding (Rawls & Bean, 2003). It begs the question, where did the city source the requisite materials for such swift reconstructions, especially when repeated several times over such a short span?

San Francisco 1850 (Notice already a lot of brick buildings)

As we go through this history, we are starting to notice some patterns. The first is that events seem out of sequence in the current narrative. The naming of San Francisco, the purchase of Alcatraz Island, and the construction methods used in Third System star forts; these all seem to have pieces of history that confirm the decisions made in some way, but the decisions themselves could not have considered this data that validate them because it occurs later in the timeline.

As an example, that we provided earlier, Sir Frances Drake probably established the name San Francisco. Where he got the name from is still open for discovery, but his voyage to the California coast and the appearance of that name on maps directly coincide. Our timings in history for the name completely align and make total sense once this is established. Without it, using the current history, the name comes too late in the timeline. It is backward. It forces us into a rabbit hole of arguing about which ancient map maker was the biggest idiot and opens the door to much confusion. We will eventually have to find a motive if all this confusion is purposeful. A thread of investigation that is emerging for us is that it seems like our current history, in many places, is utilizing a Distraction Ploy.

A Distraction Ploy is a deceptive tactic where minor errors or distractions are intentionally embedded within a larger falsehood or narrative. These intentional inaccuracies serve as "spotlights" which attract immediate attention and scrutiny. As a result, the focus is diverted away from the primary deception, causing observers to believe they are critically evaluating the information by identifying these minor inaccuracies. This grants unwarranted credibility to the more significant, overarching claim or falsehood (Ellul, 1965).

San Francisco 1853

Such a strategy is often employed in propaganda, marketing, and even academic settings when there is a desire to divert attention from a fundamental flaw or untruth (Wardle & Derakhshan, 2017). The primary and often more consequential deception remains unchallenged and is implicitly accepted by luring critics or observers into a false sense of satisfaction after spotting these minor errors.

We must adopt a holistic approach when assessing information to counteract the Distraction Ploy effectively. This is why we are using this Syntopical approach. It is the countermeasure to a Distraction Ploy. We need to move past merely identifying obvious errors; there must be a concerted effort to evaluate the foundational premise of the information critically. Such a rigorous approach demands a synthesis of detail-oriented scrutiny, as described by Kahneman (2011), coupled with a comprehensive big-picture perspective reminiscent of Postman's (1985) insights. To clarify an unrelated topic, consider a report that claims a new drug has no major side effects. If this report intentionally contains minor statistical errors, critics might fixate on correcting these statistical discrepancies. In doing so, they might overlook or fail to challenge the broader claim of "no major side effects," even if such a claim is unsubstantiated (Cialdini, 1984).

San Francisco 1856

We will find the same thing here in our history of San Francisco regarding materials in the 1850s; the sequence of events and the idea that unlimited resources were shipped in and magically unloaded and distributed, as you will see, does not make logical sense. We are mentioning this now so you can evaluate the historical narrative with a skeptical lens.

THE DISASTERS

On December 24, 1849, San Francisco was struck by the First Great Fire. The blaze originated in Dennison's Exchange, a notable gambling establishment, and quickly spread, decimating structures around Portsmouth Square (Summers, 1989). The resulting devastation was extensive, with property damage estimated at over $1 million—a staggering amount considering the economic standards of the period.

The catastrophic event left a substantial part of the city's infrastructure in ruins, necessitating urgent reconstruction. Given the primary reliance on timber as the predominant building material before the fire, its demand surged post-disaster. This is not wholly unreasonable, as, at this point, the builders did not know that more disasters were on their way. Still, with the colossal scale of damage, sourcing sufficient timber locally presented challenges. This situation led to the increased importation of timber and other necessary construction materials to facilitate the city's recovery. Simultaneously, the gravity of the disaster propelled some builders to consider bricks as a more resilient alternative for reconstruction, setting the stage for its growing significance in the city's architectural fabric (Lotchin, 1974).

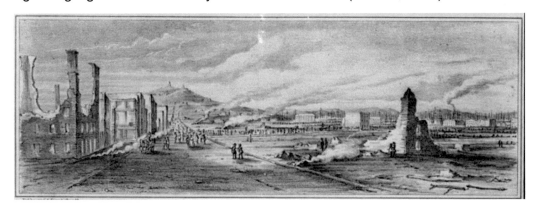

After 1851 Fire

It is essential to understand that while timber continued to be the mainstay, we are told the aftermath of the First Great Fire marked the beginning of a gradual shift towards embracing brick as a durable and hopefully more fire-resistant construction material in San Francisco's urban planning (Richards, 1987). Brick is one of the most fire-resistant building materials still in use today, so this decision makes sense, even if we learn it was ineffective for fire prevention, at least in the San Francisco of the 1850s.

Six months later, on May 4, 1850, the Second Great Fire of San Francisco wreaked havoc upon the growing city. Believed to have ignited from an improperly extinguished cigar on Kearny Street, the flames rapidly spread, consuming a significant portion of the city's structures (Dillon, 1961). Within a short span, over 2,000 buildings were obliterated. While this number of 2,000 is well documented (Dillon, 1961), given that the population in 1850 was roughly 25,000, it is hard to conceptualize that 2,000 buildings would have represented a building for every ten or fifteen people. If the entire population worked to rebuild, including women and children, one wonders where the repair and restoration labor force came from. The aftermath of the fire presented an immediate need for reconstruction, with nearly $4 million 1850s dollars in damages.

A month and a half later, on June 14, 1850, San Francisco was engulfed by the Third Great Fire, which ignited at a store on the northeast corner of Kearny and Jackson Streets (Lotchin, 1974). The rapid spread of flames wreaked havoc across a significant part of the city, culminating in an estimated monetary loss between $3 million and $4 million (Summers, 1989). The fire's aftermath was a monumental challenge for the city, which was already grappling with the need for rapid infrastructural development amidst the Gold Rush.

San Francisco Docks, 1850

Just ninety days later, on September 17, 1850, San Francisco was once again devastated by a significant blaze known historically as the Fourth Great Fire. At this point, it is impossible to conceptualize the horrors and uncertainty of living in these conditions. This time, the conflagration began in a paint and oil store on Kearny Street (Lotchin, 1974). The fire's volatile source facilitated a swift spread, destroying several city blocks. By the time the fire was under control, the damage was estimated to surpass $1 million (Summers, 1989).

On May 4, 1851, history tells us that another catastrophic event, the Fifth Great Fire, besieged San Francisco. Curiously, the date of this fire mirrored that of the second major fire and happened exactly one year later, to the day (Lotchin, 1974). This blaze initiated on the east side of the Plaza and rapidly devoured a significant portion of the city's northeastern region. In its wake, *another* 2,000 structures were reduced to ashes, with the total damage estimated at a staggering $12 million this time (Summers, 1989).

Faced with *another* monumental rebuilding task, San Francisco's need for building materials surged again. However, supposedly now focused on brick construction, the sheer magnitude of the destruction meant that sourcing sufficient bricks locally was challenging, leading to increased importation and heightened logistics.

Not to be outdone, between the fifth and sixth fire, there was an earthquake on May 15, 1851 (Toppozada, 1988) that destroyed more of the city, requiring more to be rebuilt.

On June 22, 1851, San Francisco was *yet again* ravaged by fire (it is becoming challenging to present this with a straight face), specifically the Sixth Great Fire. Its origins can be traced to a cabinet shop on the east side of Dupont Street, between Sacramento and Clay Streets (Lotchin, 1974). The flames rapidly spread, consuming 14 city blocks in their relentless path. The destruction was profound, with damage estimates surpassing $3 million (Summers, 1989).

The historical narrative has been specifically designed to convince us that San Francisco's repeated encounters with fires significantly influenced its urban development during a critical period of its history. As a result of this consistent devastation, we are given a reason for a marked transition in building materials, moving from wood to brick. This shift is meant to explain an essential aspect of San Francisco's architectural progression and why the remaining infrastructure does not have a history of progression.

Here is the basic high-level timeline we are given as the historical narrative:

1. **Emergence of Brick Constructions (1850-1851):** Post fires in the latter part of 1849 and early 1850, there was an acute realization of timber's vulnerability. By 1850, bricks began dominating the construction landscape as the city rose from the May and June fires (Lotchin, 1974). Recognized for their durability and relative fire resistance, bricks became the material of choice for many commercial buildings and establishments. Despite their higher cost and longer

construction times compared to timber, their benefits in terms of fire resistance made them a sound investment (Hansen, 2008).

2. **Bricks as the Backbone (1851-1853):** The brick's stature grew exponentially during these years. Commercial hubs were being reconstructed with brick, and residential areas also saw a surge in brick-based constructions. While advanced fire-resistant techniques were explored, such as integrating cast iron facades, the core construction still heavily relied on bricks (Cronon, 1991). Several iconic buildings from this period, some of which utilized millions of bricks in their structure, stand testament to the brick's paramount importance in San Francisco's architectural narrative.

3. **Innovation Within Brick Constructions (Post-1853):** As the city moved past the immediate aftermath of the devastating fires, builders did not merely settle for traditional brick constructions. Instead, they innovated, combining bricks with other materials like sandstone and terra cotta tiles for interiors (Issel & Cherny, 1986). This blending improved fire resistance and added aesthetic appeal to the buildings.

4. **Bricks and Building Codes (The mid-1850s onwards):** With bricks becoming synonymous with San Francisco's rebuilding spirit, the city's officials recognized their importance in the broader construction landscape. Stricter building codes of the mid-1850s advocated for fire-resistant constructions and stipulated guidelines on brick quality, masonry techniques, and structural integrity (Lewis, 2007).

We have chronicled these fires and their reconstructions to frame the local environment into which the military minds responsible for building Fort Point had stepped into, assuming this narrative is authentic. The city had burned to the ground six times in the past year and a half and had at least one substantial earthquake. Gold had been discovered two years prior, and the materials to build the city were stretched so thin that they were now importing materials from overseas while ignoring local resources like granite quarries (as we documented prior). Bricks are used in such volume that it is incredible, but prominent local historically known brick manufacturers do not appear on the scene for another two decades.

Something needs to be added up. Let's dive into some of the logistics concerning bricks. Let's clean the term up also; what do we mean when we say "brick"? What is involved in creating these materials, and what would the early 1850s San Francisco have looked like to truly meet this demand?

A FOCUS ON BRICK AND ASSOCIATED RESOURCES

Does the narrative concerning San Francisco as it grappled with a series of fires between 1849 and 1851 add up? The history is an intricate series of unfortunate events that seem designed to justify the city's architecture and construction choices that we can see today. The history seems to follow the Distraction Ploy methodology we identified in the prior section. We will lay out the reality's of 1850s logistics here.

The narrative would have us believe that amidst the fiery backdrop just described, brick emerged as the principal material for reconstruction, driving significant demand for related resources and labor. Once again, this analysis seems backward. The city is built of brick, so we are told that the decision was made to use brick, even though the reality is that the amount of brick used would not have been available at the time. The local brick capabilities arrived in the 1870s, but much of the work is already done by then. Here, we will attempt to unravel the complexities of this reconstruction period, emphasizing the various components integral to brick-based architecture.

Battery & Washington circa 1856

The narrative says that the aftermath of San Francisco's series of fires brought to light the apparent vulnerabilities of wooden structures. With an acute awareness of this susceptibility, San Francisco's architecture shifted to brick construction. This pivot increased the demand for bricks significantly.

The primary component of brickmaking is clay. Fuel was another indispensable component of the brick-making process. Coal or wood was the primary fuel source to fire the bricks and convert damp, molded clay into sturdy, fire-resistant building blocks. The trade networks of the time, such as the coal imports from Vancouver Island in British Columbia, facilitated the coal supply for various industries, including brick kilns (Lotchin, R. W., 1974).

Old City Hall 1856

Sand, an often-underappreciated component in the brick-making process, was essential for the firing stage. By scattering sand on the kiln's floor, brickmakers ensured that the molded clay bricks would not adhere to the surface during firing, ensuring the bricks' integrity and uniformity. Also, sand is used in the actual bricks themselves. These materials and processes would have formed the backbone of San Francisco's brick supply chain, responding to a pressing demand from the city's tumultuous relationship with fire.

However, a wall is not built from brick alone; brick construction necessitated using mortar, a material critical for binding bricks together and ensuring structural stability. Mortar production during this vast rebuilding phase hinged on several of its own core ingredients.

Lime, often used as a binding agent in mortar, was derived from heating limestone. This heating process transformed limestone into quicklime, which, when combined with water, resulted in slaked lime. When mixed with sand, this substance became the chief component of mortar. The limestone used for this purpose in San Francisco during the mid-19th century was likely sourced from quarries in the Santa Cruz Mountains, which were known for their rich limestone deposits (JRP & Associates, 1998).

Sand, like in the bricks themselves, was essential for giving volume and texture to the mortar and was another key ingredient. Water, the final ingredient, was indispensable in achieving the appropriate consistency for the mortar. It activated the binding properties of lime, creating a malleable paste that could adhere to bricks effectively. Together, lime or cement, sand, and water comprised the trinity of mortar production.

The demand for structural reinforcements became pronounced as San Francisco embarked on rebuilding with more multi-story brick structures. Bricks alone could not bear the stress of taller buildings. Iron and steel beams, known for their strength and resilience, were introduced into construction to provide the necessary support.

Iron, accessible from the iron mines in the Sierra Nevada region, was integrated into the city's architectural designs (Bancroft, 1890). These beams provided horizontal support to distribute the weight of brick walls and floors above and offered resistance against the city's infamous seismic activities.

Furthermore, the cohesion of these brick structures was enhanced using metal ties embedded within the brickwork at regular intervals. They linked the walls together, ensuring an integrated strength. Anchors, crucial to the structural integrity, held external walls to the main edifice, preventing potential outward collapses. Roofing materials played a pivotal role in rebuilding San Francisco after the fires. Brick tiles were an evident choice, harmonizing with the city's newfound preference for brick walls. Their fire-resistive nature made them integral to the city's rebuilding strategy. Slate, another durable and fire-resistant material, started gaining traction as a roofing choice. Predominantly sourced from quarries in Vermont and Pennsylvania (Conard, 1980).

Foundations were pivotal in ensuring the stability and longevity of the brick structures erected in San Francisco. Granite, recognized for its inherent strength and durability, was a primary material choice for this foundational work. Sourcing granite from China is noteworthy in the city's building history (Tsai, 2004). When aware of the Distraction Ploy, though, this narrative is almost certainly untrue, at least at any scale. However, it is a very forceful element of the San Francisco narrative. In dealing with the Distraction Ploy, this item also established physical ties to materials from Asia. Hold onto this notion, as we will revisit it later. It is important.

However, for now, it is just a noteworthy out-of-place element. We will continue with the historical narrative. The process of laying foundations demanded a precise set of tools. Picks and chisels were indispensable for the shaping and fitting of granite blocks. Ensuring that the foundation layers were aligned and accurate involved using plumb bobs, spirit levels, and string lines. Furthermore, the task of positioning each stone perfectly called for mallets, wedges, and pry bars.

Sansome & Washington circa 1858

Attention to detail and functionality characterized the interiors of San Francisco's post-fire buildings. Plaster was commonly applied to the walls, providing a consistent and paint-ready surface with the added advantage of being fire-resistant (Douglas &

Rischel, 2004). Plaster and mortar are close enough in materials that we do not need to break plaster down but simply recognize that it put an even heavier burden on the materials supply chain.

Timber remained a significant component inside these structures. Despite the vulnerabilities of wood in the face of fire, it was still a preferred material for interior use. Timber beams were integral to structural support, while hardwood floors were desired for their durability and visual appeal. Moreover, timber was used in interior partitions, delineating spaces and creating rooms as required (Glass, 1992).

Old Customs House circa 1855

The importance of natural lighting in interior spaces meant that glass became another vital material. The need for windows in the city's rebuilt structures would have necessitated an increase in local glass production or importation to meet the demand (Poppeliers, 1983).

It is hard to see tradesmen eager to design the glorious interior spaces given the fact that the city was destroyed every few months, but nevertheless, we are told that all this advanced artisanry was the standard of the day. Brick edifices, touted as fire-resistant answers in the wake of the fires, were confronted with their susceptibility to earthquakes. Considering the earthquake, builders, and city officials had to address a twofold challenge: the pressing need to swiftly reconstruct post-fire damage while ensuring these new edifices could withstand the seismic challenges inherent to San Francisco's geolocation.

Nevertheless, where was all this money coming from? Just like Fort Point, it is difficult to conceptualize that people were building these monumental works of brick while simultaneously dealing with devastation on a scale rarely seen on the world's North American stage and competing with the military for resources, all with a population lesser than what today in North America we consider a small town.

Here is a summary of the costs to repair the fires, as presented:

Date	Fire Name	Estimated Cost (1850s)	Estimated Cost (2023)
Dec 24, 1849	First Great Fire	$1 million	~$50.5 million
May 4, 1850	Second Great Fire	$4 million	~$202.2 million
June 14, 1850	Third Great Fire	$3-4 million	~$176.9 million (average)
Sep 17, 1850	Fourth Great Fire	$1 million	~$50.5 million
May 4, 1851	Fifth Great Fire	$12 million	~$690.4 million
June 22, 1851	Sixth Great Fire	$3 million	~$172.6 million

Based upon this analysis, the military leaders who decided to build Fort Point in the Third System style had opted for an 8-million brick structure on the rocky peninsula breakwater at a time when all bricks were made by hand in an environment close to the aforementioned apocalypse. In all its infancy, the burgeoning city had just seen seven catastrophic events over a year and a half (six fires and a major earthquake), equal to damages of roughly $1.5 Billion in today's dollars adjusted for inflation. Our analysis suggests that rebuilding San Francisco seven times over in today's dollars would be hundreds of times more expensive than simple inflation.

We are told the population at the end of 1852 was 34,776 (Eldredge, 1912). Given all this rebuilding and the planned Fort Point project, what percentage of the population would have needed to be directly employed in construction?

1850s BRICK-MAKING LOGISTICS

The history is just so impossible at this point that it feels like we are piling on, but we have yet to organize the analysis to get anything close to an accurate picture of 1850s San Francisco. When we push aside all the fanciful and whimsical stories about the 1849 gold rush, we are left with a burgeoning city that might not have been able to produce the structures we are told were built, certainly not in the timeframe or with the resources available to them. We will work to understand what this could mean, but before that, we must finish organizing the history to understand where it is fragmented.

It is hard to get your head around, but the 1.5 billion dollars in repair work is just the beginning of the construction. We are told the city built massive new buildings between 1853 and 1862, when Fort Point, the "strategic key to the Pacific west coast," was being constructed. These new buildings would have been competing for resources with Fort Point, and, as we are detailing, San Francisco was already stretched thin concerning resources, which begs the question, what about labor?

All this 1850s construction work, and all of these bricks, were made prior to brick-making machinery innovations, which were still thirty or so years away (Harris, 2006). In an analysis of brick production in the 1850s, we are dealing with hand-formed bricks; understanding the volume yield is crucial. Drawing upon the standardized dimensions of such bricks from this period—8.5 inches in length, 4.5 inches in width, and 2.5 inches in height—one can calculate the volume of an individual brick to be approximately 95.625 cubic inches (Houben & Guillaud, 1994) of raw materials per brick. When juxtaposed with the known measurement of 1,728 cubic inches in a cubic foot (Tatum, 2005), roughly 18 bricks could theoretically be derived from a cubic foot of raw material.

However, considering the inefficiencies inherent in the manual production processes of the era, not all raw material is utilized optimally. A conservative estimate suggests a wastage rate of 25%, attributable primarily to molding losses and firing imperfections (Campbell, 2006). Factoring in this wastage, the accurate yield approximates 14 bricks per cubic foot of raw material. This quantification offers a realistic perspective on the resource demands of 1850s brick-making practices.

An in-depth analysis of San Francisco's reconstruction endeavors during the 1850s post-fire phase indicates a pronounced demand for bricks, as we have proven. While it is impossible to form perfect numbers, based on the above data, we estimate that the city needed approximately 200,000 bricks a day from 1852 to 1861. Based on the dimensions and volume calculations of 1850s handmade bricks (above), this translates to an estimated 22,180 cubic feet of raw material each day, assuming an average yield of 13.56 bricks per cubic foot after accounting for production inefficiencies. We will provide our calculations for this in a subsequent section by comparing known annual brick production in later decades based on the brick-making companies that do eventually form in Northern California.

For now, using simple math, we will assume that on a day of perfect productivity by the most skilled brick molders of the day, 2,000 bricks could be molded by a worker (Campbell, 2006). However, one single brick molder requires a tremendous amount of infrastructure and support. It may require twenty to thirty workers in different roles to support one molder producing 2,000 local bricks daily. Where a Brick Molder was a skilled worker who molds clay into bricks, the support roles included:

1. **Raw Material Gatherers**: Workers responsible for sourcing and collecting clay and other necessary materials from local deposits, ensuring a consistent supply for brick production.

2. **Clay Preparation**: Individuals tasked with preparing the clay for molding. This involves removing impurities, grinding the clay to the correct consistency, and adding water or other additives to make it pliable for molding.

3. **Molding Assistants**: Assistants who help prepare molds, supply clay, and stack formed bricks for drying. Their support ensures that the brick molder can work efficiently.

4. **Drying & Firing**: Personnel who manage drying the formed bricks in the sun or in a drying shed and subsequently firing them in a kiln to harden.

5. **Transport**: Workers responsible for the movement of raw materials to the manufacturing site and transporting finished bricks to storage or to customers.

6. **Other Support Roles**: Miscellaneous roles might include clean-up crews, helpers for various tasks, and other supportive positions not explicitly defined.

7. **Buyer/Purchaser**: The individual in charge of establishing relationships with suppliers, negotiating prices, and purchasing necessary raw materials.

8. **Inventory/Warehouse Manager**: Oversees raw materials and finished bricks storage. They ensure optimal utilization of storage space and maintain a record of inventory levels.

9. **Warehouse Workers**: Individuals responsible for handling materials and finished bricks within the warehouse, including stacking, organizing, and retrieving bricks as needed.

10. **Shipping Coordinator**: Manages the transportation logistics for distributing bricks to customers, coordinating with external transportation providers or overseeing an in-house fleet.

11. **Administrative Assistant/Clerk**: Handles clerical tasks such as invoicing customers, tracking payments, and maintaining records.

12. **Quality Inspector**: Ensures that bricks meet established standards, checking for consistency in size, shape, and overall quality. They work closely with molders and the firing team to address quality issues.

13. **Security Guards**: Protect the facility and stored bricks from potential theft or vandalism, especially if bricks are stored in accessible outdoor areas.

14. **Manager/Supervisor**: The individual overseeing the operation, ensuring coordination between various roles, and making managerial decisions to optimize production.

15. **Equipment Maintenance Team**: Responsible for the upkeep of any tools, molds, kilns, and other equipment, ensuring everything functions optimally and safely.

Also, note the storage requirements and the tonnage of raw and finished materials that would have needed to be moved each day. In manufacturing bricks, particularly using traditional methodologies, the selection and proportion of raw materials are of utmost significance. The primary ingredient is clay, which exhibits a density ranging from 63 to 78 pounds per cubic foot (Mitchell, 1993). To prevent shrinking and cracking during the drying process, sand, having a density fluctuating between 90 to 100 pounds per cubic foot (Lambe & Whitman, 1969), is integrated into the clay mixture.

Handmade Bricks, Stacked. Modern.

To produce a durable brick, more clay than sand is generally used. If, hypothetically, the blend constituted 75% clay and 25% sand, this would produce an average estimated density of around 71.75 pounds per cubic foot for the mixture. A daily raw material volume of 22,180 cubic feet would equal a daily weight close to 1,592,110 pounds, or approximately 796 tons. This is, however, a rough estimation. Deviations in the specific blend ratios or variations in the types of clay or sand used can result in different weights.

Modern Brick Pallets

In 1850s San Francisco, the horse-drawn wagons, commonly tasked with transporting goods, were limited not so much by their inherent design but rather by the city's rudimentary infrastructure. The roads of the era—often muddy, unpaved, and fraught with congestion (when not on fire)—served as tangible constraints on the amount of weight a wagon could reliably transport (Lotchin, R. W., 1974).

By conservative estimates, based on historical records, the wagons could bear a burden of approximately 1 ton per trip (White, J. H., 1978). Given these conditions, transporting 796 tons of raw materials would require a minimum of 796 individual wagon trips. When accounting for the finished bricks, this number effectively doubles (transport raw materials in and finished bricks out), reaching a sum of 1,580 trips, as the finished bricks must be moved a second time from production to construction. Given that there are 1,440 minutes in a day, this means a new trip for a brick wagon every 54 seconds.

However, taking these figures at face value would be imprudent without considering the broader logistical challenges. The stated 1-ton capacity is merely a theoretical upper limit, and the actual operational efficiency was invariably lower. The frequent bottlenecks on San Francisco's busy thoroughfares and the challenges posed by muddy and uneven road surfaces (Dillon, R. H., 1999), could easily impede transportation. As such, while the arithmetic might suggest 1,580 trips a day, the practicalities of navigating 1850s San Francisco's challenging landscape imply that a much higher number of trips—or a more significant commitment of time and resources—would likely have been necessary.

In our analysis, all of this seems to rule out local brickmaking—the historical narrative we are given supports our view. The San Francisco region, including its surrounding Bay Area, was not characterized by significant commercial clay deposits ideal for brickmaking. The geology of the immediate San Francisco vicinity is more dominated by materials like sandstone, serpentine, and shale rather than expansive fields of brick-making clay (Kyle, 2002).

In our exploration of the brick-making boom of the 1850s in San Francisco, it is worth noting that while there were areas in California known for their extensive clay deposits, they were not immediately tapped for the city's construction needs. Lincoln, California, situated in Placer County to the northeast of Sacramento, is a prime example. This region boasted some of California's most expansive clay deposits. However, significant enterprises capitalizing on these resources, like Gladding, McBean & Co., only emerged in 1875 – over two decades after the 1850s boom. While this company, renowned for its terra cotta products among others, highlights Lincoln's rich clay resources, it underscores that these were not the immediate source of materials for San Francisco's mid-century brick demand (Ferrero, H. (1998).

Again, the history is out of order.

Also, the volume of bricks and resources might seem overstated. However, there is a historical context to support our analysis, both in the volume of bricks needed and in the unavailability of finished bricks until very late in this 1850s boom cycle. Remember, we are still dealing with the compressed timeline for the construction of Fort Point, which, to make the probably already impossible construction timeline, would have needed eight million bricks starting in the early 1850s when the granite foundation made from imported Chinese materials was completed.

For domestic brick production, which demonstrated the Fort Point narrative is impossible while also supporting our estimates concerning the number of bricks San Francisco needed daily, we are told that by 1864 (two years *after* the completion of Fort Point), the combined efforts of the Remillard brothers resulted in the establishment of the Remillard Brick Company in what was then known as Brooklyn (present-day part of Oakland). After mastering brickmaking in Boston, Hilaire (often known as Philip-Hilaire) Rémillard arrived in California in 1854. His initial foray into mining near Auburn was driven by the aim of accumulating finances to bring his brothers, Pierre-Nicolas "Peter" and Edouard "Edward" Rémillard, to the Golden State. The company quickly gained prominence in the brick-manufacturing sector. By 1879, they boasted an annual production of 45 million bricks (123,000 a day), supported by an extensive workforce of 400 employees (San Francisco Call, 1904). The challenge for us is that this is well past the time period we are interested in (the narrative is in the wrong order). Also, note that the Remillard Brick Company was one of four or five brick establishments with this output level, we are told, to emerge as the 19th century ended. This means that by 1879 San Francisco was locally producing roughly a million bricks a day.

However, that is two decades later, according to the narrative. In the 1850s, where did all the bricks come from? We are told they were imported.

If we revisit our Chinese granite calculations, remember that we concluded that about 400 tons was the average complement of a cargo vessel. Moreover, separately we have calculated the 200,000 daily bricks to their tonnage of 768 tons. To deliver this tonnage, there would need to be two fully loaded cargo vessels a day for bricks for the entire duration of the 1850s.

While the details will elude us as the narrative does not address any of this, unloading 400 tons, given the conditions and number of workers, could take weeks. Given the constraints of multiple daily cargo ships, it could take much longer, but anything less than two weeks seems unrealistic. So even if we assume perfect conditions for every single shipment, we will have two ships a day moored for at least 14 days, or a total of 28 ships moored and being worked constantly for the entire nine years of construction for Fort Point. It takes longer when you factor in the six fires, earthquakes, and general growth.

Moreover, we have not even gotten to the fire of 1906, when we are told everything was destroyed and rebuilt.

Again.

But that is for later.

Sticking to our analysis period focused on the construction of Fort Point, the picture of San Francisco painted is a hell on earth of logistical impossibilities.

Nevertheless, we are told that the most influential military minds of the day decided to implement a Third System fort on the west coast, critical to the emerging nation's national defenses, in preparation for an impending civil war, on a rocky peninsula jutting out as a breakwater, in a bay that had only been named in 1775, seventy-five years prior, and into an environment so resource constraints and so fought with natural disaster that one wonders how any analysis of the situation could have suggested any measure of success.

CHAPTER 5: TRANSITIONING TO PRIMARY SOURCES

BRINGING ORIGINAL ANALYSIS INTO THE CONVERSATION

PRIMARY SOURCES

On some level, we are falling right into the Distraction Ploy. We are mucking through details, working to realign them to support the current historical narrative. It is a deceptively simple trap that aligns well with the human psyche; we feel a sense of satisfaction proving the narrative wrong, missing the overarching point that we are working at such a micro-level that our arguments, in the long run, are tactically appropriate but strategically irrelevant.

The Distraction Ploy capitalizes on human cognitive tendencies to focus on immediately noticeable details, often at the expense of the broader truth or deception. The intentional inaccuracies serve as "spotlights," luring observers into a trap where they believe they are critically evaluating the information. By identifying these minor inaccuracies, the observer may feel satisfied with their analysis, overlooking the primary deception. This can occur in various forms of communication, including political discourse, advertising, literature, and more.

With its structured and comprehensive approach to information examination, Adler's Syntopical Analysis (Adler & Van Doren, 1972) offers a powerful countermeasure to the Distraction Ploy.

The first step of syntopical analysis involves identifying and selecting the relevant works or sources contributing to the subject. We have started to do that from a literary standpoint. However, this topic struggles with a purely literary analysis because the history we are dealing with is so convoluted, and almost all literary sources, at this point, are secondary sources.

Primary sources are firsthand, original documents or evidence relating to a specific event, topic, or period. These sources are produced by those who directly witnessed or participated in the phenomenon being studied, providing direct access to the event or subject in its original form (Library of Congress, n.d.). Primary sources present raw, unmediated information that allows researchers to engage directly with the subject. In Adler's Syntopical Analysis framework, primary sources furnish the essential data needed to grasp the core of the subject, and when applied to combat the Distraction Ploy, they enable a clear and direct understanding (Adler & Van Doren, 1972).

Secondary sources are not firsthand; they are interpretations, analyses, or evaluations of primary sources and offer secondhand perspectives of the original data. Secondary sources contribute valuable context and commentary to primary information, synthesizing and critiquing the raw data. Within Syntopical Analysis, they help create a comprehensive analysis, blending different viewpoints and insights (Adler & Van Doren, 1972).

The nuanced relationship between primary and secondary sources is integral to scholarly investigation and particularly relevant within Syntopical Analysis. Syntopical Analysis achieves a complex, multi-faceted comprehension of a subject through the thoughtful integration of both source types. This methodology is especially pertinent in navigating intricate information landscapes and in countering deceptive tactics like the Distraction Ploy, furnishing a resilient method for critical thinking and analysis. However, it is not easy work as this encompasses not just traditional texts but also images, digital content, literary works, or conversations. For instance, if analyzing a particular theme in art, this stage would require selecting pertinent paintings, sculptures, or photographs from different artists. This stage's essence lies in identifying sources that will offer diverse perspectives on the subject.

We need to shift our analysis from secondary to primary sources and expand to other types of artifacts like images and photos. The critical steps we need to follow, according to Adler (1972):

1. **Broad and Deep Engagement with Sources**: Syntopical Analysis encourages a broad and deep engagement with various sources, fostering a holistic understanding of the subject. By comparing and contrasting different perspectives, it inherently promotes a focus on the broader context rather than isolated details. This can help recognize and bypass the intentional inaccuracies that form part of the Distraction Ploy.

2. **Analyzing Terms and Problems**: Emphasizes the analysis of key terms and problems across different sources. This critical examination goes beyond surface-level distractions to uncover underlying themes and issues. It helps recognize the larger narrative or falsehood the Distraction Ploy may conceal.

3. **Constructing a Dialogue among Sources**: By bringing various sources into the conversation, Syntopical Analysis encourages an evaluation of different viewpoints. This interconnected analysis safeguards against being misled by individual distractions, as the focus remains on understanding the complexities and intricacies of various perspectives.

4. **Synthesis and Comprehensive Understanding**: The final stage of constructing a syntopical analysis involves synthesizing insights from various sources into a coherent whole. In our work, this coherency will need to start to drive us to a rational of an accurate narrative, and it must also start to drive us to some semblance of understanding a motive for the fragmentation of history. This process minimizes the risk of being trapped by the Distraction Ploy, as it emphasizes the integration of diverse perspectives, making it difficult for minor inaccuracies to divert attention from the main subject.

The Distraction Ploy represents a cunning manipulation of human attention and critical evaluation, employing minor inaccuracies to divert scrutiny away from a primary deception. Mortimer J. Adler's Syntopical Analysis, emphasizing holistic understanding, critical examination of terms and problems, and synthesis of various viewpoints, is an effective counterbalance to this deceptive tactic. By fostering an analytical mindset that transcends surface-level distractions, Syntopical Analysis offers a robust methodology for navigating the complexities of modern information landscapes, where deceptive practices like the Distraction Ploy may be increasingly prevalent. Its applicability across different mediums and subjects further underscores its value as a versatile critical thinking and analysis tool.

This section of the analysis will exclusively utilize primary sources to conduct a historical and geographical study of early San Francisco, specifically focused on our subject matter, the feasibility of the Fort Point construction narrative set against the historical backdrop of the time. To do this, we will utilize a surveys from the years 1849 and 1859, visual records captured in images from the 1850s, and contemporary digital tools such as Google Maps and Google Earth.

The 1849 survey (Eddy, 1849) directly accounts for San Francisco's state at that time, offering firsthand insights. The images from the 1850s provide authentic visual documentation of specific phases in the city's progression. Through contemporary tools, Google Maps and Google Earth offer primary data on the present-day geographical landscape.

Utilizing Syntopical Analysis to examine these primary sources allows for a precise and rigorous examination of San Francisco's transformation over time. The method facilitates the critical juxtaposition and analysis of these materials, unveiling connections, contrasts, and underlying patterns in the city's development.

This analysis's emphasis on primary sources underscores our commitment to academic rigor and integrity. It ensures the study is grounded in firsthand evidence, fostering a detailed and authentic understanding of the subject. This alignment with primary sources extends the applicability of Syntopical Analysis, demonstrating its versatility in handling different types of original materials, ranging from historical documents to modern digital platforms.

1. **Survey Accuracy:** The 1849 survey's alignment with the technological capabilities of its time will be analyzed by comparing its precision with contemporary understanding and historical documentation of surveying techniques.

2. **Temporal Discrepancies in Images:** The images will be scrutinized by examining architectural records, dates, and other historical data to identify potential inconsistencies related to the claimed dates of construction.

3. **Alignment with Contemporary Views:** The study will use Google Maps and Google Earth to correlate historical visual records with present-day geographical representations, identifying continuities and discrepancies.

Applying Syntopical Analysis in this context involves a rigorous cross-examination of these sources, probing their interrelations and contrasts. It will engage with:

- **Viewing and Interpretation:** The images will be closely viewed and interpreted to grasp their contextual meaning, visual elements, and relevance to the subject of investigation.

- **Identification of Key Visual Themes:** Visual themes, patterns, and motifs will be identified across the images, providing a unified framework for analyzing the visual narrative and stylistic choices.

- **Comparison and Contrast of Visual Elements:** The visual elements, such as composition, iconography, and spatial organization within the images, will be critically compared and contrasted. This comparison will shed light on similarities, differences, and potential incongruities within the visual records.

- **Analysis of Visual Discrepancies:** Any visual incongruities or impossibilities within the images will be meticulously analyzed. This examination will involve understanding the historical context, architectural features, geographical alignment, and technological insights pertaining to the time when the images were created.

- **Synthesis of Visual Insights:** Insights gathered from the viewing, comparison, and analysis of the images will be synthesized to present a coherent understanding of the visual narrative or to raise further questions related to visual accuracy, representation, and historical interpretation.

Through this methodical and systematic approach, the ensuing investigation seeks to uncover potential inconsistencies or impossibilities within the historical record.

1849 OFFICIAL SURVEY OF SAN FRANCISCO

Urban development and spatial organization are subjects that have been systematically studied through the utilization of primary sources such as maps and surveys (Harley, 1987). A significant example in this regard is the Official Map of San Francisco by William M. Eddy in 1849, which provides crucial insight into the historical geography of the city (Eddy & Graham, 1849). This survey delineates San Francisco's streets, lots, and public spaces. However, the technological advancements in modern mapping allow us to ask questions regarding the survey's accuracy.

The analysis commences with an engagement to grasp the survey's contextual meaning and relevance. By carefully interpreting the visual elements of the survey, a more profound comprehension of its historical significance emerges. Within this framework, the focus shifts towards identifying key visual themes and patterns within the survey. Such themes are discerned through detailed observation and are subsequently contrasted with contemporary satellite imagery, providing a touchstone for comparison.

Next, the intricate process of comparison and overlay comes into play. Here, the historical survey and modern satellite maps are meticulously juxtaposed, a procedure that emphasizes visual similarities and differences. This exacting comparison allows for a critical assessment of the survey's accuracy. Attention is concentrated on the alignment or deviation between the mapping forms, offering unique insights into San Francisco's geographical landscape.

Following this comparative exercise, an investigation into visual similarities or discrepancies is undertaken. This phase of the analysis requires a rigorous examination of consistencies or inconsistencies. By utilizing technological insights, a reasoned judgment on the survey's accuracy is formed. Every visual cue is dissected and evaluated in light of its historical context and present-day representation.

Concluding the process, the gathered insights are integrated. This synthesis, formed through critical observation and technological assessment, either affirms the survey's historical precision or raises further inquiries regarding its representation. The final synthesis encapsulates a coherent understanding of the survey, integrating historical authenticity with modern mapping technology.

KEY 1849 MAP FEATURES

1849 W. M. Eddy Survey

There are several elements to dissect from this historical document.

First, the 1849 survey of San Francisco presents an offset grid pattern extending 6,000 feet by 12,000 feet and representing over 3,000 addressed segments within the grid where tens of thousands of buildings stand within this grid today. The precision and complexity of this survey, conducted by William M. Eddy, elicit both admiration and skepticism, particularly when examined in the context of the historical backdrop.

San Francisco was then a burgeoning city, as we have already covered at length. It witnessed exponential growth primarily due to what we are told was the California Gold Rush. However, the vast and intricately detailed grid pattern depicted in the survey appears incongruent with the city's then-modest population and chaotic construction climate. Records indicate that San Francisco's population in the late 1840s was estimated to be under 400 people until the last two years of the decade (Lotchin, 1974), which hardly justifies such an extensive and systematic urban plan.

Moreover, the timing of the survey aligns with a transitional phase in California's history, one of many. Conducted in 1849, the survey predates California's admission to the Union as a state, which occurred in 1850. The planning intricacy and the scale of the urban design depicted in the survey seem somewhat premature, considering the political uncertainty and the embryonic stage of the state's governance structures.

Furthermore, San Francisco's foundation as a chartered city dates to only April 15, 1850, a year *after* the survey was conducted. The map represents quite a fantastic settlement, given that this was before incorporation. The founding of San Francisco on April 15, which would become Income Tax Day in America, seems tongue-in-cheek to us. Additionally, given the city's formal establishment stage, the ambitious grid system raises real questions concerning the necessity and feasibility of such an advanced planning strategy. In assessing the 1849 survey, a discerning eye is required to reconcile the apparent contradictions between the highly detailed urban plan and the contextual realities of the time. The questions posed by this analysis engage directly with historical accuracy, alignment with demographic data, political climate, and the technological capabilities of the era.

This Official Map of San Francisco provides a striking representation of a city that, in certain aspects, diverges from the historical context of the time. Specifically, the survey's depiction of the shoreline with the known geographical features of the period, but the anomaly lies in the portrayal of the city's grid extending well into the water in certain places.

This extension of the city grid into the water is a curious observation, as it aligns with the final city layout that eventually emerged over 150 years later through extensive land reclamation projects. However, these developments were far in the future, well beyond the purview of the surveyor, William M. Eddy, in 1849. The city of San Francisco was in its emergent stages, and California was on the cusp of statehood. The notion that a survey from this time would so closely represent the future layout of the city is a perplexing inconsistency.

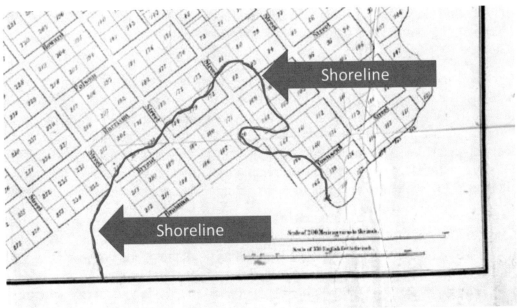

The specific alignment of the city grid with future developments appears anomalous. It raises fundamental questions: How could the 1849 survey reflect the intricacies of urban expansion that occurred over the subsequent centuries? What factors might explain this unexpected correspondence between the survey and the eventual city layout?

These questions do not undermine the survey's validity but instead contribute to an enriched and nuanced understanding of this historical document. By meticulously examining these peculiarities and considering them within the broader historical and geographical context, a more comprehensive insight into the early urban planning of San Francisco can be achieved.

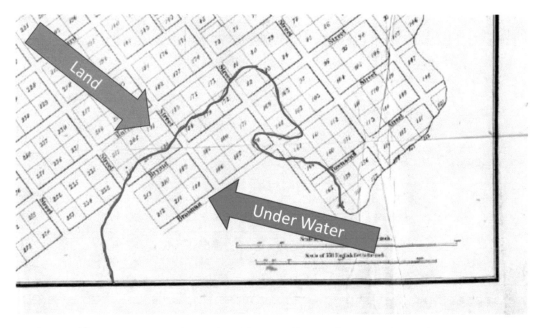

A specific mapping tool provided by the David Rumsey Map Collection's online platform was employed (David et al., 2023). This tool facilitated an intricate overlaying of the historical survey with current satellite imagery, enabling a precise comparison between the past and present. The following sets of images are from this tool and show a modern map overlayed on the 1849 survey map.

A significant visual clue emerged when conducting this overlay. Streets such as Bryant Street and Brannan Street that were depicted in the underwater portion of the 1849 survey aligned exactly with their current locations in 2023. These streets, seemingly submerged in the past, now correspond with reclaimed land. This alignment is not only exact but is corroborated by the historical survey and the current satellite imagery available through the mapping tool.

This discovery raises a puzzling question central to our analysis: How could the 1849 map maker have known the precise alignment and layout that would only become apparent after extensive land reclamation projects that were completed over a century later?

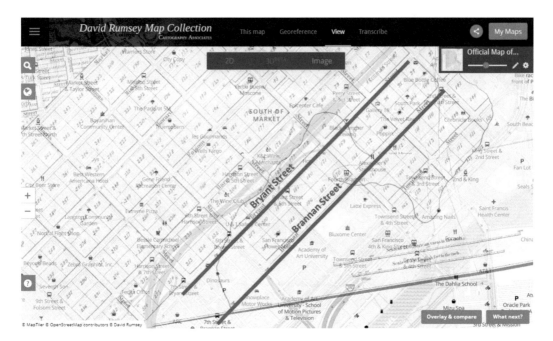

This alignment between past and present, particularly highlighted by the exact location of streets like Bryant and Brannan, is a compelling discovery.

How were surveys like this 1849 one created? What tools were available at the time?

The 1849 San Francisco survey opened a window into the techniques and tools employed by surveyors during this historical period. A skeptical examination of this survey inevitably leads to an inquiry into the methodologies that would have been utilized during that time. How was such an extensive and detailed map produced with the tools and techniques available in the mid-19th century? What does the method of surveying reveal about the intriguing details found within the map, such as the alignment of certain streets?

In the 19th century, surveying was a complex and demanding task requiring mathematical knowledge, technical skill, and physical labor. The process typically involved two-person crews using linked chains to measure distances (Linklater, 2002). These chains were carefully calibrated, and the surveyors would physically extend them across the land, taking meticulous measurements to map the terrain.

This chain method required careful attention to detail and significant manual labor, as the landscape itself often posed significant challenges. Hills, valleys, water bodies, and other natural features must be considered. Accuracy depended heavily on the expertise of the surveyors, the quality of their equipment, and the conditions in which they were working.

One of the most prominent tools of the time was the theodolite, an instrument used for measuring angles in horizontal and vertical planes (Peterson, 1995). Surveyors could create a highly detailed and accurate landscape representation by combining the angular measurements taken with the theodolite with the distances measured using chains. However, these measurements were far from trivial to perform, requiring substantial expertise and precision.

Antique Theodolite

In the context of 1849, a survey accurate to within an inch over a 6,000 by 12,000-foot area would indeed be a formidable task. The complexity would be very high using the tools of the time, including the theodolite for angle measurements and chains for distances (Peterson, 1995).

Assuming an angular resolution of one second (a typical accuracy level for theodolites of the time) and considering the need to measure over varying terrain with many different points to survey, a typical observation might take anywhere from a few minutes to several hours.

The distances, too, would need to be measured with utmost precision, given the accuracy requirement of one inch. Measuring a single line could take a day or more, depending on the method and terrain. Now, for a 6,000 by 12,000-foot area, and assuming a grid pattern with a survey point every 100 feet (a typical interval for detailed surveys), there would be 720,000 individual points to measure.

Assuming an optimistic average time of one hour per point, which is very generous as there would be additional time to break down and set up the equipment for each measurement, the total time required would be 720,000 hours. If a two-man team worked 10 hours daily, five days a week, the required time would be nearly 140 years. If Eddy, the surveyor, worked 24 hours a day for seven days a week, he could have cut this time nearly in half and only would have taken 82 years.

Please do not dismiss this observation, as we will demonstrate that this survey is accurate to within an inch of the current 2023 buildout of San Francisco.

Considering the level of detail in the 1849 San Francisco survey, the surveyors must have applied fantastical techniques with exceptional skill. Also, again, remember that this survey is so accurate that it mapped hundreds of feet of future land underwater with correct street names and address blocks; the depiction of a detailed grid extending even into the water, along with the exact placement of streets like Bryant and Brannan, reflects a level of precision and prediction that invites puzzlement.

In assessing the 1849 survey of San Francisco, particular attention must be given to the meticulous detail with which angles were mapped, especially in the case of Market Street. This thoroughfare, significant in its length and complexity, provides a unique case study in understanding the precision and craftsmanship of 19th-century surveying techniques due to its angle in the grid.

Market Street presents a divergent angle that cuts through the city grid, creating an intricate geometry that poses significant challenges in mapping. The degree of precision required to accurately map such a complex angle is not trivial, even by modern standards. However, the 1849 map exhibits astonishing accuracy, aligning with the city's current 2023 layout to within mere inches.

Such an exact similarity begs the question: How was this accomplished using 19th-century surveying techniques?

To answer that question, we must acknowledge that achieving such accuracy with the technology of the time would have required more than just the right tools; it would have necessitated exceptional skill, judgment, and a profound understanding of geometry and trigonometry. The mathematical calculations required to translate the raw measurements into an accurate representation of Market Street's divergent angle would have been a complex undertaking; the surveyors would have had to balance the demands of accuracy with the realities of a dynamic and evolving urban landscape.

The precision with which Market Street's complex angle was mapped in the 1849 survey adds another layer of intrigue to our analysis. The alignment of this historical mapping with modern satellite imagery to within inches reflects a level of technical prowess that challenges our understanding. The lingering questions and anomalies associated with this mapping seem to point to certain impossibility.

Also, worth pointing out, is that this survey is taken pre-great-fires and earthquakes. This means the city was surveyed, then burned to the ground something like ten times (we have covered the first six so far), rebuilt each time, and the survey is still, in many places, within an inch or two of the modern day.

The 1849 San Francisco survey analysis reveals a remarkable phenomenon that defies easy explanation. The implications of this accuracy extend across the entire survey. Streets such as Broadway, Vallejo, and Green, and cross streets like Taylor, Mason, and Jones all appear to align within feet of their current counterparts, intersecting with the exact same centers as they do today. This alignment is observed not just in a single isolated instance but across the entire mapped area, reinforcing an astounding pattern of precision.

The survey presents an anomaly that is difficult to reconcile with our understanding of historical methods and capabilities. The logical explanation that a modern reader might seek is not readily apparent within the confines of the documented techniques and tools of the period.

What, then, are we to do with this survey?

Who is enforcing these building codes when there are no city ordinances for another three or four years?

How can we reconcile the chaotic, hastily built wooded structures that will start burning down later in the year?

Is the narrative that almost a thousand people a week are flooding into San Francisco, building temporary structures but being sure to only build in a grid pattern?

Can all this simply be dismissed as a fabrication, or does it challenge our assumptions about the capabilities of 19th-century surveyors?

What other possible explanations might there be?

A possible answer to these questions will reveal itself as we conduct further research and reflection. It will not involve a claim of forgery concerning this survey or rely on some convoluted explanation about American Exceptionalism, nor some fanciful planning ability that never existed.

Nevertheless, returning to this analysis, our study of this survey underscores the importance of approaching historical documents with an open mind and a critical eye. The 1849 San Francisco survey provides a case study of the complexities of historical analysis, where seemingly straightforward primary sources can reveal unexpected and potentially paradigm-shifting insights.

We know no possible explanation for an official 1849 survey showing San Francisco essentially as it is mapped out today in 2023. We will try not to repeat ourselves, but looking back to the prior chapters as we chronicled the living hell that was San Francisco of this time period, we find it impossible to believe that in 1849, a grid system of thousands of buildings was built out within the course of a year, then mapped to such a precision that street names, including streets originally mapped as being underwater, should still exist to within a foot or less in 2023, in some cases within an inch or two of today.

We believe the only explanation is that the chronology for San Francisco that we are given in the historical narrative and that we have documented already from glowing peer-reviewed secondary sources needs to be corrected. To what degree and to what outcome, we have yet to determine. However, we must review more primary sources before considering a more formal conclusion.

UNITED STATES COAST SURVEY, 1857

The 1857 U.S. Coastal Survey map of San Francisco, published in 1859 under the supervision of A.D. Bache, presents a peculiar conundrum. The map reveals an 80-foot sand dune on Market Street just west of Kearny and 3rd Streets, an anomaly that starkly contrasts the surrounding urbanized landscape (United States Coast Survey, 1859).

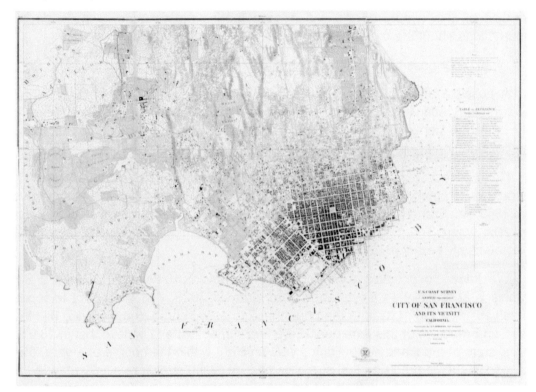

1859 Survey

The existence of a large sand dune on Market Street during this period raises questions, as it contradicts the broader narrative of urban development reflected in the rest of the map. Mainly east of the future site of Union Square, the map indicates an advanced state of urbanization. Streets, including St. Mark's Place, had been graded and constructed, and an alley had been transformed into an actual road. Even Geary and Post Streets were shown as being cut and graded almost up to what was then identified as the Public Square. This level of development suggests that the region was transitioning from a natural landscape to a structured urban environment.

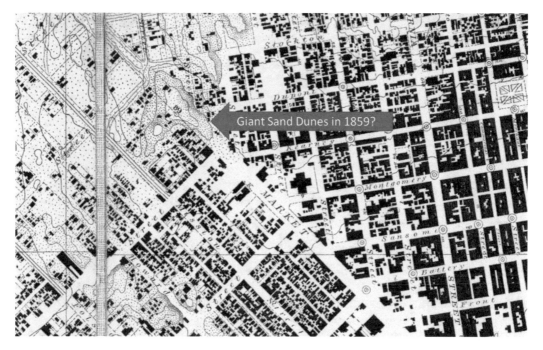

Zoom in on the 1859 Survey

However, sand dunes, particularly the 89-foot dune on a primary thoroughfare like Market Street, create a puzzling juxtaposition. Sand dunes are typically associated with undeveloped, natural landscapes and are not features commonly found in urban settings, especially not on main streets that are otherwise shown as part of a graded and developed urban grid. The dune interrupts the logical flow of urban development and raises questions about the accuracy of the map or the understanding of the city's topography at that time.

The anomalous presence of a large sand dune on Market Street amidst signs of substantial urban development presents a historical and geographical puzzle in direct conflict with the Eddy survey map we just examined, supposedly created in 1849.

It seems that things continue to be in the wrong order. Wouldn't the sand dunes have been cleared *before* building Market Street under them? How can the Market Street grid still be perfect under the sand dune? How was it even measured?

FORT POINT, 1856

During our investigation into Fort Point's historical background, a significant aspect that caught our attention was the construction timeline from 1853 to 1861. A meticulous analysis of the schedule was undertaken, wherein we allocated a period of two to three years specifically for the acquisition and installation of the Chinese granite foundation.

Even with generous assumptions, we concluded that it was plausible, though highly dubious, for the foundation of a structure of Fort Point's magnitude to be completed within two years. This assessment considers the availability of resources and labor, which were elements we scrutinized in our analysis.

This interpretation pushes the boundaries of our otherwise rigorous and objective approach, aligning closely with an almost liberal assessment of the feasibility of such a construction timeline. Nonetheless, it is crucial to stress that we intend to approach this study with a sense of impartiality, avoiding undue biases and, therefore, providing a well-balanced analysis. Thus, our generosity in these calculations is guided by our commitment to maintaining an unprejudiced perspective on the historical data available.

HV-5 from 1856

With the foundation completed in 1855, we are given six years for the rest of the construction in the narrative we have previously provided. In the Eddy (1849) survey, we also have a picture of how built out and organized San Francisco was in 1849.

In the process of scrutinizing Fort Point's construction timeline, a puzzling visual artifact has surfaced that challenges the conventional historical narrative. A photograph from 1856, captured during what was understood to be the brick phase of Fort Point's construction, shows Fort Point already completed, and yet, without a flag flying, an indication that it had not yet commenced its military function.

What deepens this mystery is the stark absence of any signs suggesting recent construction. A project as substantial as Fort Point would have required comprehensive infrastructure, including roads for transporting materials from nearby ports. Such a network is conspicuously absent in the photograph. Furthermore, the lack of visible scaffolding and the absence of ships or boats in the bay around the fort, which would have been expected during construction, calls into question the authenticity of the accepted timeline.

The image's foreground adds to this conundrum, appearing too primitive to correspond to San Francisco's landscape in 1856, especially in light of the detailed 1849 survey and other cataloged visual records from that era.

Rather than merely presenting a historical discrepancy, this photograph seriously calls into question the accepted historical narrative of Fort Point's construction. The glaring lack of evidence for recent construction, the unexplained absence of maritime support, and the inconsistency of the surrounding landscape with documented visual depictions of the area all cast significant doubt on the conventional understanding.

The analysis of this specific visual artifact not only underlines the essential role of visual evidence in historical investigation but also exposes potential weaknesses in the accepted historical narrative of Fort Point's construction. Far from suggesting that additional analysis may be required, this investigation points to a more profound and unsettling conclusion: the current historical account may be fundamentally flawed.

The image serves as a vital piece of evidence, necessitating a reevaluation of previously unquestioned assumptions and an acknowledgment that our understanding of the past may not be as secure as previously believed. It is not merely a question of aligning this image with the existing historical record; instead, it may require a thorough reexamination of the entire historical framework surrounding Fort Point's construction.

This deeper skepticism towards the accepted narrative underscores the historical investigation's complexity and critical nature. It highlights how a single image can open new paths of inquiry, prompting a reassessment of long-standing historical interpretations. By exploring the anomalies within this photograph, we uncover the often-fragile nature of historical understanding, reminding us that history is not a static construct but a dynamic and contested field of study.

If this photograph shows there were some components of San Francisco already present before their construction dates, are there other photos with similar data?

1851 MERCHANT EXCHANGE BUILDING

Battery & Washington circa 1856 (Build 1851)

The narrative surrounding the construction of the original Battery Street Building in San Francisco in 1851 raises intriguing questions that warrant scholarly skepticism, particularly when considering the historical context of the city's development. The edifice, described as a three-story brick structure with sophisticated internal functions, ostensibly positions itself as an architectural marvel, as can be seen in the above image. This portrayal seems particularly puzzling when evaluated against the myriad of challenges facing San Francisco during this period, including natural disasters like fires and an earthquake and logistical and resource constraints (Wilson, 1994).

Just think about the idea of constructing this building while dealing with the threat of fires and earthquakes. It's truly a remarkable architectural achievement. However, it starkly contrasts the "quickly built wooden structures" that are clearly visible nearby, down the road.

There is very little information available from primary sources about this particular building. It's mentioned briefly as a side note because it once served as the location of the United States Courthouse for a few years before the court was moved two blocks away (Wilson, 1994).

While the Battery Street Building is often praised for its architectural and functional excellence that reflects San Francisco's business aspirations, a closer examination reveals inconsistencies that challenge this narrative. The grandeur attributed to the building, the choice of materials for its construction, and the ambitious timeline for its completion seem at odds with the broader historical and logistical context of early 1850s San Francisco.

View from Sansome Street 1858

We challenge this narrative as we cannot find a realistic path to this building, having been constructed between 1849 and 1851, given our prior analysis. The building in the image to the Exchange's right side would be a stretch given the narrative, but at least it is in a block architectural style that could, with generosity, have emerged during this time period. However, for the Exchange, what laborers would have been pulled off the massive reconstruction projects of the time.

EVIDENCE OF THE OLD WORLD

Remember, six disasters, destroying thousands and thousands of buildings; who was it that was hoisting up Greek statues and plumbing intracite pillars and arches instead of helping rebuild the devastation?

CHAPTER 6: WORLD FAIR'S

IT'S A SMALL WORLD AFTER ALL

While we have been focused on San Francisco in the 1850s and earlier, it is crucial to periodically examine tangential worldwide events that may provide more insights into the time period, following the syntopical methodology and approach.

This chapter will introduce the World's Fair concept and provide its generally accepted history alongside skeptical viewpoints that have gained traction over the years. We aim to furnish a balanced narrative, focusing on events on the timetable associated with our interest in San Francisco. The skepticism we note in this section is just for completeness; we are not claiming them nor disavowing them, simply making you aware of them so you have the broader context.

On the one hand, World's Fairs, known variously as Expositions Universelles or International Expositions, are often hailed as grand public exhibitions that have been instrumental in shaping international relations, fostering innovation, and molding cultural identities since the 19th century. These events are credited with being platforms where countries can present their technological advancements, cultural heritage, and potential future developments on an international stage (Auerbach, 1999; Findling & Pelle, 2008).

On the other hand, a skeptical lens invites questions about the undercurrents and possible hidden agendas behind these spectacular events. Some theories suggest that the fairs were platforms for promoting covert ideologies or establishing a new world order. Such theories often point to these events' organized, grandiose nature, positing that they were tools for indoctrination. For instance, the "White City" concept introduced at the 1893 Chicago World's Fair has been scrutinized as a potential attempt to subtly introduce and normalize specific social or political agendas (Larson, 2003).

Further skepticism surrounds the logistical aspects of these fairs, especially the rapid construction and subsequent demolition of elaborate buildings and artifacts. Theories speculate that this could indicate hidden technologies or lost ancient knowledge. While mainstream historical accounts contend that these structures were intentionally temporary due to financial and logistical constraints, alternative theories question whether there might be more to the story (Findling & Pelle, 2008).

Notably, the first significant World's Fair in the United States was the Centennial Exposition of 1876 in Philadelphia, a critical juncture for a nation grappling with the aftermath of the Civil War and Reconstruction. The exhibition is traditionally seen as a symbol of national unity and technological progress (Rydell, 1984). However, the inception of the World's Fair concept can be traced back to national and regional exhibitions that set the groundwork for later international events. Although smaller-scale exhibitions occurred before the 19th century, such as the Society of Arts Manufactures and Commerce in Britain during the 1750s, the fairs took on an international dimension and greater public prominence beginning in the 19th century (Auerbach, 1999).

The evolution of World's Fairs into the 20th century reflects technological innovations and ideological shifts, encapsulating the aspirations and anxieties of their respective times (Findling & Pelle, 2008).

The Crystal Palace, 1851

The 1851 Great Exhibition in London serves as an important milestone. Organized by Prince Albert and Henry Cole, the exhibition took place in the Crystal Palace, an architectural marvel made of iron and glass. Known for its international scope and emphasis on industrial technology and design, this exhibition set a precedent for subsequent World's Fairs (Auerbach, 1999). Despite its celebratory tone, skeptics have questioned whether the event consolidated Britain's imperial and industrial powers, effectively shaping a narrative that supported the status quo.

Exposition Universelle of 1867

Following the London exhibition, several other significant World's Fairs took place, including the Exposition Universelle in Paris in 1867. This event was notable for introducing new inventions like the sewing machine and reinforcing Paris's role as a center of culture and innovation.

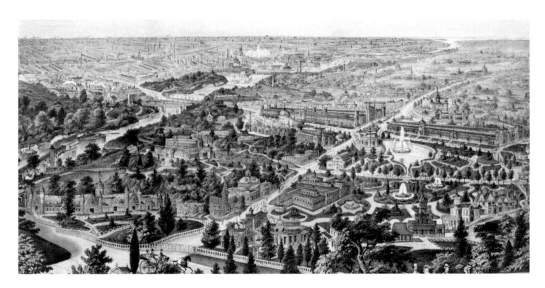

Centennial Exposition of 1876

Another key fair within our period of interest is the 1876 Centennial Exposition in Philadelphia, commemorating 100 years since the American Declaration of Independence. As mentioned, this was the first major World's Fair in the United States. This exposition showcased innovations like the typewriter and telephone (Rydell, 1984).

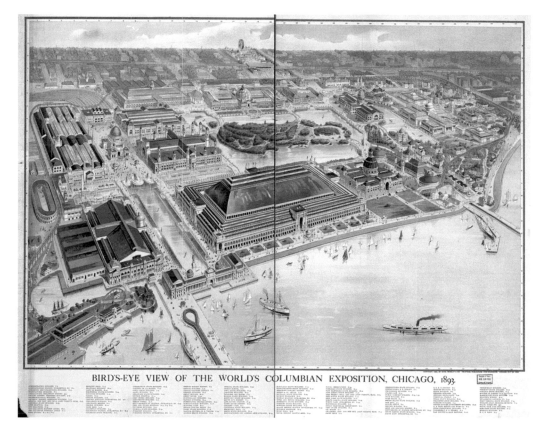

BIRD'S-EYE VIEW OF THE WORLD'S COLUMBIAN EXPOSITION, CHICAGO, 1893.

1893 World's Columbian Exposition

Further on, the 1893 World's Columbian, celebrating the 400th anniversary of Christopher Columbus's arrival in the New World; the fair is famous for its "White City," innovations like the first Ferris Wheel, and its influence on urban planning and architecture (Larson, 2003).

Finally, the 1894 California Midwinter International Exposition in San Francisco. This exposition holds a unique place in the history of World's Fairs and is particularly relevant given its location in San Francisco's Golden Gate Park. Its timing, coming a year after the immensely influential 1893 World's Columbian Exposition in Chicago, also positions it within a continuum of American and international exhibitions that aimed to showcase progress, culture, and innovation (Findling & Pelle, 2008).

OFFICIAL BIRD'S-EYE VIEW OF THE CALIFORNIA MIDWINTER INTERNATIONAL EXPOSITION
SAN FRANCISCO CALIFORNIA

1894 California Midwinter International Exposition

Conceived by M. H. de Young, founder of the San Francisco Chronicle, we are told the 1894 Midwinter Exposition was designed to boost the local economy and elevate the city's national and international profile. In many ways, it succeeded, drawing millions of visitors to experience the exhibits, cultural displays, and amusement rides. Unlike the grandiose World's Fairs in Chicago, Paris, or London, we are told the Midwinter Exposition was a smaller affair but still showcased significant achievements in the fields of art, industry, and agriculture (Baddeley & Baddeley, 1894). The event also presented California as a land of opportunity and abundance, reinforcing notions of the American West as a frontier for progress and prosperity. Promotional materials and exhibits highlighted California's natural resources, cultural diversity, and potential for economic development, weaving a narrative aimed at attracting settlers, investors, and tourists to the region (Todd, 1894).

We will undoubtedly return to each of these fair locations in future research where we can do our breakdown of materials, time, and labor. For now, we will outline the significant fairs leading up to the San Francisco fair and then dig into that fair in more detail.

1851 GREAT EXHIBITION IN LONDON

The historical narrative surrounding the 1851 Great Exhibition, organized by Prince Albert and Sir Henry Cole, often speaks of its tremendous scale and impact on industrialization and international diplomacy (Auerbach, 1999; Leapman, 2001). Set in London's Hyde Park within the groundbreaking Crystal Palace, we are told that the exhibition drew over six million attendees during its 90-day run. While this figure has been widely cited, a skeptical lens prompts further questions about the reported attendance numbers and the logistical arrangements that such a massive event would necessitate.

Dickinson's Comprehensive Pictures of the Great Exhibition of 1851 - 1

The claim of six million attendees over 90 days, which averages to approximately 67,000 visitors per day, presents several logistical enigmas when considered within the context of 19th-century infrastructure and technology. One of the immediate questions that arise is the housing arrangement for this influx of visitors. London in 1851 needed to be equipped with the sort of mass accommodation facilities we associate with modern cities. So, where did all these people stay? What lodging was available, and how could these facilities accommodate such a significant population surge? These concerns, often unaddressed in traditional accounts, raise questions about the logistics of hosting an event of this magnitude (Hobhouse, 2002; Greenhalgh, 1988).

Crystal Palace 1851

Similarly, the matter of food for the attendees deserves scrutiny. The average diet and the availability of cuisine in 1851 London were significantly different from what we are accustomed to today. So, what did these six million attendees eat? How did these vendors manage to source and supply food for such a large and diverse crowd? The historical records seldom probe into seemingly mundane but critical details, thus leaving a gap in our complete understanding of the event (Leapman, 2001; Hobhouse, 2002).

Entrance to the Egyptian Court

Crystal Palace, Egyptian Court, 1851

The speed with which the Crystal Palace was reportedly assembled —under nine months—also warrants further examination, given the available construction technology of the era (Auerbach, 1999; Hobhouse, 2002). Coupled with this is the complexity of organizing a global exhibition featuring contributions from various countries, a feat that would be incredibly challenging even today due to logistical and diplomatic complexities (Greenhalgh, 1988; Leapman, 2001). It is hard to imagine managing the buildout while simultaneously coordinating with attending countries and exhibitors. How were they convinced the fair would take place on time? How would you line up hundreds of countries and thousands of vendors without the confidence of completed infrastructure?

While the 1851 Great Exhibition is undeniably a landmark event in the history of World's Fairs, adopting a skeptical perspective uncovers a series of unanswered questions. These questions, mainly related to logistics like housing and food for the attendees, the astonishingly rapid construction timeline of the Crystal Palace, and the complexities of organizing such a large-scale international event, introduce a layer of intricacy often missing from mainstream narratives. Such scrutiny serves not to discredit historical accounts but to enrich our understanding by revealing the gaps and challenges that are often left unexplored in the existing literature.

Dickinson's Comprehensive Pictures of the Great Exhibition of 1851 - 2

EXPOSITION UNIVERSELLE OF 1867

The Exposition Universelle of 1867, held in Paris, is another significant milestone in the chronology of World's Fairs. Historically, this event has been celebrated for its global outreach and the introduction of several innovations. Conceived as a grand showcase of industrial progress and cultural exchange, we are told that the exposition attracted more than 15 million visitors over its duration from April to November (Mattie, 1998; Haupt, 1972). Organizers presented this as a triumph of modern civilization, emphasizing the collaborative spirit of different nations coming together in a single platform (Haupt, 1972; Greenhalgh, 1988).

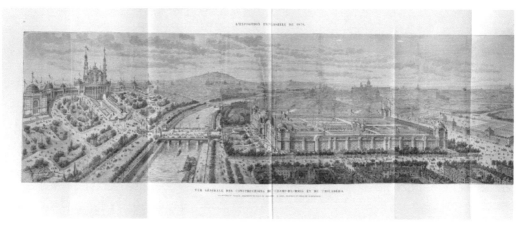

Panoramic view of the 1878 World Fair

However, if over 15 million people visited the event during its operation, it raises the same essential questions like those prompted by the 1851 Great Exhibition. Specifically, one must ask: where were these visitors accommodated? What did they eat? Given the urban constraints of Paris at the time and the limitations in mass housing infrastructure, this vast number of visitors would have presented a substantial logistical challenge (Mattie, 1998; Haupt, 1972).

The rapid development of the exposition's infrastructure also merits closer inspection. It is recorded that more than 50,000 exhibitors participated in the Exposition, necessitating a vast area for display (Mattie, 1998; Haupt, 1972). The structure reportedly sprawled across the Champ de Mars, covering 119 acres. Given the engineering and architectural tools available in the mid-19th century, the speed and efficiency with which this space was organized and erected could be seen as either an extraordinary accomplishment or a point requiring further critical examination (Haupt, 1972).

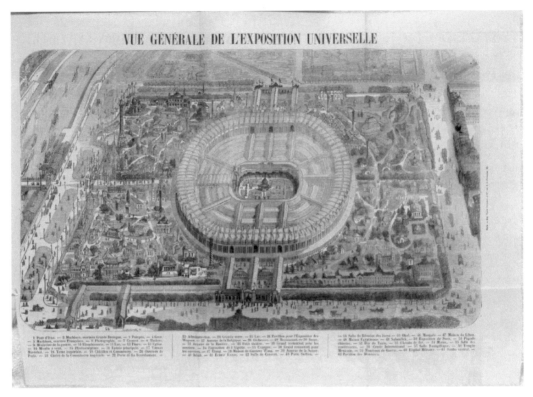

Exposition Universelle of 1867

The Exposition Universelle of 1867 remains an iconic event, acclaimed for its impact on industrial advancements and international relations. However, a cautious review reveals several logistical questions that are rarely addressed in conventional accounts. These questions concern the provision of accommodations and food for an influx of millions and the incredibly rapid construction and organization of the exhibition space. Scrutinizing these dimensions offers a more nuanced understanding of the challenges and intricacies of organizing an event of such immense scale. The gaps in the existing narrative, while not discrediting the importance of the Exposition, invite us to probe for a more profound and complete understanding of its true history.

CENTENNIAL EXPOSITION OF 1876

Opened in Philadelphia from May 10 to November 10, 1876, the exposition reportedly drew nearly 10 million visitors, further accentuating the logistical marvel and challenges the fair presented (Wilson, 2016; Gross & Harris, 1981). As always with the fairs of this time, given the short build times, massive volume of attendance, and six-month duration, the construction process of the Main Exhibition Building is one facet of the elaborate logistics of making the Centennial Exposition a reality that warrants skepticism.

This exposition's Main Exhibition Building, constructed predominantly of glass and iron, covered an expansive area of over 20 acres, which was an unprecedented feat at the time and was hailed as the world's largest building (Rydell, 1984; Gross & Harris, 1981).

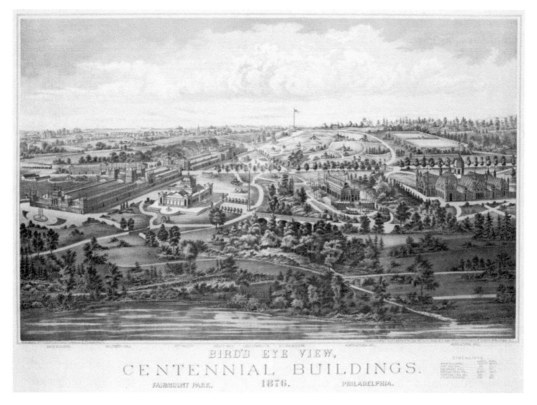

Centennial Exposition Of 1876

Another complex aspect was procuring and transporting the vast quantities of glass and iron needed for the main building (Wilson, 2016). These materials had to be sourced, often from distant locations, and transported to the construction site, which undoubtedly presented its own set of logistical hurdles. Given the limitations of the era's transportation technology, the swift coordination and transportation of these materials would have required extraordinary planning and execution.

Corliss Engine, Main Exhibition Building

The financial landscape of the Centennial Exposition is another arena that invites scrutiny. A project of this magnitude would have required substantial financial resources. Various funding sources, including governmental agencies, private corporations, and public contributions, were orchestrated to pool the necessary finances (Gross & Harris, 1981). The complexity of managing such a diversified portfolio, especially considering the speed at which the whole thing was put together, begs the question of how effectively the exposition's finances were administered.

The Centennial Exposition of 1876 in Philadelphia occupies a significant place in historical discussions for its iconic status and the grand scale on which it was executed. However, it's crucial to examine the logistical and financial intricacies of its planning and execution. From constructing the world's largest building to the intricacies of material sourcing and financial planning, the exposition raises several questions that demand a deeper, more nuanced analysis.

Agricultural Hall at Centennial Exposition, 1876

1893 WORLD'S COLUMBIAN EXPOSITION

Grand Basin of the 1893 World's Columbian Exposition

The 1893 World's Columbian Exposition, also known as the Chicago World's Fair, was meant to celebrate the 400th anniversary of Christopher Columbus's arrival in the New World, although it was held a year late, opening on May 1, 1893, and closing on October 30, 1893. Regarding attendance, reports indicate that over 27 million people visited the fair during its six-month duration (Rydell, 1984; Wilson, 2016).

The fair's planning and execution involved extensive buildings and exhibits spread across nearly 700 acres. The grandest of these was the "White City," a complex of neoclassical buildings designed by people we are told were some of America's most prominent architects at the time. The claim is that buildings were constructed primarily with a combination of plaster, cement, and jute fiber to simulate the look of marble, and the largest among them was the Manufactures and Liberal Arts Building (Harris, 1993; Larson, 2003). It was claimed to be the largest building in the world at that time, covering approximately 44 acres.

Chicago Aerial View, 1893

The rapid construction of the "White City," with its elaborate designs and extensive footprint, brings forth specific skeptical considerations. With the era's technology, one naturally questions how such massive structures could be erected relatively quickly. Furthermore, the production and transport of the materials used—such as plaster, cement, and jute fiber—would have been a substantial logistical endeavor, given the technology available in the late 19th century (Harris, 1993).

The use of "staff," has been skeptically discussed, especially since "staff" was a cutting-edge technology at the time, having only been invented in the 1850s. We are told the material was designed to be temporary and less expensive than traditional building materials like stone or brick. However, the grand appearance of these structures, particularly their striking resemblance to marble, has led to some skepticism about how such an elaborate and aesthetically impressive cityscape could be erected in a short span of time with what was essentially a form of 'faux' construction material (Harris, 1993; Larson, 2003).

View from Woman's Building, World's Columbian Exposition, 1893

Critics and skeptics often point to the impermanence of "staff" as indicative of the temporary nature of the fair itself, especially "staffs" inability to work against water, yet if the narrative we have is true, then there are many images of "staff" doing fine with water. Additionally, one might question the logistical aspects of producing enough "staff " to cover the large surface areas of the multiple grand buildings. With the technology of the late 19th century, this material's mass production and application for a project on the scale of the World's Columbian Exposition became subjects warranting further scrutiny (Harris, 1993).

Financially, the fair was a complex venture involving a mix of federal appropriations, municipal bonds, and private investment, including corporate sponsorships and individual donations (Rydell, 1984). The administrative complexities of managing such diverse funding sources within a limited timeline pose their own questions. It adds another layer of curiosity about how financial planning was executed so successfully in an era without the advantages of modern communications and tools.

MacMonnies Fountain and Machinery Hall, 1893

The 1893 World's Columbian Exposition remains a central event in world fairs and American culture history. While its grandeur and impact are well-documented, the logistical and financial intricacies behind its quick construction and large-scale operation raise questions that demand closer scrutiny. As always, we are not presenting these observations to diminish the event's historical significance but, instead, to add depth to our understanding of the immense challenges the organizers would have faced if the narrative for this fair were indeed genuine.

U.S. Government Building, 1893

In summary, each of the World's Fairs examined in this chapter—London's Great Exhibition in 1851 to the Exposition Universelle of 1867 in Paris, the Centennial Exposition of 1876 in Philadelphia, and finally, the World's Columbian Exposition of 1893 in Chicago—offers a distinctive lens through which to scrutinize the logistical, architectural, and financial feats of the time. While all these fairs have earned iconic status for their grand scales, ambitious scopes, and contributions to technology and culture, they also invite skepticism when one considers the practical challenges involved in their planning and execution.

The Great Exhibition in London was revolutionary for introducing the Crystal Palace, a massive glass and iron structure, but the short planning and construction timeline raised questions about the logistical viability of the endeavor. The Exposition Universelle of 1867 in Paris extended the trend of monumental exhibitions and brought with it its own complexities, especially regarding the construction timeline and materials used. Philadelphia's Centennial Exposition featured what was then the world's largest building and raised questions about the logistics of material sourcing and financial planning. Finally, the 1893 World's Columbian Exposition in Chicago was a marvel of aesthetics with its White City and a subject of controversy around the use of temporary materials like "staff" while managing to, yet again, construct the world's largest building, topping the prior Philadelphia fair.

While a monumental achievement, each fair presents practical complexities and questions that warrant a more nuanced understanding.

CHAPTER 7: 1894 MIDWINTER
INTERNATIONAL EXPOSITION IN SAN FRANCISCO

1894 MIDWINTER CONTEXT

This chapter offers a conventional historical narrative of the 1894 California Midwinter International Exposition, also known as the Midwinter Fair, based on information collected from well-known secondary sources. The objective is to present a thorough and traditional account as has been historically understood, with a specific focus on the economic dimensions of the event. In this chapter, we lay the groundwork for a foundational understanding of the fair, avoiding overly critical scrutiny or probing too deeply into the inconsistencies in the prevailing narrative beyond some simple math and rudimentary observations.

We will dig deeper, but first, the story as offered should be presented.

Administration Building

That said, we do believe it is fundamental to note that the chapter following this one will diverge from this approach. Utilizing primary sources in the next chapter, we will analyze more rigorously, scrutinizing the details and offering alternative viewpoints based on our own conclusions. This may present a narrative contradicting the conventional understanding established through these secondary sources. Do not view this as a conflict but a refinement; this chapter serves as an introductory exploration that sets the stage for a more nuanced and potentially challenging discussion to follow.

To begin, then, we are told that this 1894 event was conceived to bolster the city's economic and cultural profile. Opening its doors on January 27, 1894, and running until July 4 of the same year, the fair spanned a total of 159 days ("America's Best History," 2023). It was a remarkable platform that showcased the diversity and achievements not only of America but also of 38 international participants. Occupying 200 acres and constructing over 120 buildings in what is now known as Golden Gate Park, the fair was a colossal undertaking in terms of logistics and financing.

Manufactures and Liberal Arts building and the Electric Fountain, 1894

The financial aspects of such an event are critical to understanding its long-term impact and feasibility. According to historical records, the total cost of organizing the fair amounted to $1,193,260.70 ("America's Best History," 2023). As for the revenue streams, the narrative says they came primarily from ticket sales. Adult tickets were priced at 50 cents, and child tickets were at 25 cents. A season pass, offering 100 admissions, was available for $40. Additionally, there were discounted pricing options for Sundays and late afternoons.

To conduct a detailed financial analysis, we need to make certain assumptions. Given that there were 1,315,022 paid visitors, let us assume that one child attended for every two adults. This would indicate that approximately 438,341 of these were children, with the remaining 876,681 being adults.

Calculating the revenue generated from adult ticket sales, we have 876,681 adults at 50 cents each, totaling $438,340.50. For children, 438,341 tickets at 25 cents each yield $109,585.25.

Fine Arts Building at 1894

Another significant source of revenue comes from season passes. If 5% of the attendees purchased a season pass at $40, then about 65,751 visitors would have contributed $2,630,040 in revenue from this avenue alone.

Adding these amounts together, we get a total revenue of $3,177,965.75. At first glance, this amount appears to significantly surpass the total cost of organizing the fair, thus suggesting that the event was financially successful.

However, it is crucial to consider the costs associated with staffing the event in addition to its construction and organizational costs of $1,193,260.70. We are told 742,399 staff and employees were needed across the fairgrounds and hundreds of vendors from the 38 countries represented. Assuming an average daily wage of $2 per employee based on historical wage data (Margo, 2000), and if we presume that

10% of this workforce was active each day for the 159 days of the fair, the total labor cost would be about $23,772,000.00.

When we account for these labor costs, the total expenses would far exceed the revenue generated from ticket sales and season passes. The shortfall suggests that, although the fair was an important cultural and social event, it was likely not a financially successful endeavor. We mention this now so you understand the broader realities given the narrative we will provide.

In comparative numbers, a loss of $23,772,000 in 1894 would be a loss of about a billion 2023 dollars adjusted for inflation.

A staggering sum if the intent (as the narrative tells us) was to bolster local economies.

Agricultural and Horticultural Hall, 1894

We are told that this exposition was a temporary attraction and, at the same time, a strategic initiative to achieve multiple objectives; predominantly, the fair sought to bolster tourism during the city's economically sluggish winter months, showcase California's bounty of natural resources and to reinforce San Francisco's emerging status as a preeminent American city (Harris, 1993).

One wonders how much additional tourism was needed to address the nearly $24 Million loss.

This financial shortfall begs mention, particularly when contextualized within the broader economic conditions of California and the United States at the time. For some perspective, it was not until two decades later, in the early 20th century, that California's Gross Domestic Product (GDP) surpassed the $1 billion mark, propelled by industrialization, the opening of the Panama Canal in 1914, and the discovery of oil in Signal Hill in 1921 (Mauer & Yu, 2007; Rintoul, 1976). The growth was also influenced by the rapid development of the film industry in Hollywood (Bordwell & Thompson, 2010).

Although it is challenging to pinpoint the exact year California's GDP crossed this threshold, it is reasonable to infer that this occurred sometime between the late 1910s and early 1920s—a far cry from our 1894 date of such an expenditure.

Thus, the economic capacity of California was significantly smaller during the time of the Midwinter Fair in 1894, making the financial losses even more striking. Even though California would go on to experience substantial economic growth in the early 20th century, the nearly $24 million loss from the fair would have been a significant burden for the state in the late 19th century. This sizable financial loss, coupled with the then-prevailing economic conditions, underscores the event's economic audacity and the risks undertaken by its organizers. Considering that the United States was also grappling with the Panic of 1893, a severe economic depression that impacted the entire country, including California, the fair's losses take on an even graver tone (Higgs, 1992), making the bizarre historical positivity seem out of place.

Mechanical Arts Building, 1894

The Panic of 1893 was a seminal economic event in the United States that had far-reaching repercussions for the financial markets and everyday life. This severe economic downturn was triggered by a combination of factors, including the collapse of railroad overbuilding and shaky railroad financing, which set off a series of bank failures. The crisis led to widespread unemployment, with estimates suggesting that around 20% of the workforce was unemployed at the peak of the depression. The panic also incited a series of events that led to social unrest, notably the Pullman Strike of 1894. Businesses shuttered, credit markets froze, and thousands of people were left jobless and homeless. The psychological impacts of the panic resonated across the nation, leading to a loss of faith in the economic system and increased scrutiny of the capitalist structure (Kindleberger, 1978; Higgs, 1992).

Mechanical Arts Building viewed from Bonet's Electric Tower, 1894

Under a cloud from the Panic of 1893, this financial shortfall should overshadow the fair; it should be reported as a folly of colossal proportions, leading to the ruin of its backers and setting San Francisco back decades in commerce.

Nevertheless, instead, we are given an illogicality. The Midwinter Fair represented a paradox in a society already grappling with the consequences of a significant financial crisis. On the one hand, it was a monumental effort aimed at economic revival through the promotion of arts, culture, and technology; on the other hand, it was a glaring example of financial overreach, occurring at a time when economic resources were already stretched thin. When considered against the backdrop of the Panic of 1893, the fair's economic failure reflects the vulnerabilities and challenges that characterized this period of American history.

Why this grave failure is not present in the following narrative is confusing, at best.

One last element to be considered as the official narrative is provided is the labor force. The estimated population of San Francisco in 1894 was around 298,000, a figure derived from U.S. Census data for the year 1900, which recorded 298,997 residents in the city (U.S. Census Bureau, 1900). When contrasted with the reported attendance figures for the Midwinter Fair—approximately 1.47 million paid and free visitors, along with 742,399 staff and employees, totaling around 2.22 million—the numbers raise several questions that warrant highlighting.

- Firstly, the logistical challenges of accommodating a visitor number that far exceeds the city's population would be immense. Even if one were to assume that visitors did not all attend at once and some were day-trippers, the hospitality infrastructure in terms of hotels, inns, and other lodging options would be stretched thin. It becomes imperative to question where all these visitors stayed during their visit to the fair.

- Secondly, the labor force reported for the fair is striking. A staff and employee count of 742,399 is nearly three times the population of San Francisco at the time. One wonders where this extensive labor force was sourced from. Was it local, or were workers brought in from other regions? Furthermore, if so, how were they accommodated in a city already teeming with visitors?

- Thirdly, the fair's timing coincided with the economic downturn triggered by the Panic of 1893. Considering the financial constraints and reduced mobility the general populace would be experiencing, the high attendance figures become even more perplexing. It is essential to consider how over a million people managed to travel to San Francisco, especially in an era when the Panama Canal had not yet been built, potentially making transcontinental travel more arduous and expensive.

These questions do not aim to undermine the historical narrative but rather invite scrutiny and a deeper investigation. In subsequent chapters, we will sift through primary sources to gain insights that might counter the established narrative presented through secondary sources. Such an approach may offer a more nuanced understanding of the fair's complexities and its place in history. But first, the official narrative.

1894 MIDWINTER FAIR OFFICIAL NARRATIVE

CENTRAL AND NORTHERN CALIFORNIA. ROUMANIAN CAFE. FRENCH RESTAURANT
MUSIC PAVILION. JAPANESE VILLAGE.
THE ADMINISTRATION BUILDING, PLAZA AND FOUNTAIN.

Administrative Building & Fountain, 1894

Conceived and orchestrated by Michael H. de Young, a prominent publisher and influential civic figure, the fair was held from January to July of 1894. It was strategically located in Golden Gate Park, an area that would subsequently benefit from the infrastructural and architectural enhancements catalyzed by the exposition (Cohen, 2005). In addition to de Young, several other influential individuals played pivotal roles in the fair's organization. One such person was M. H. de Young's brother, Charles de Young, who co-founded the San Francisco Chronicle with him. Although Charles was assassinated in 1880, the newspaper remained an influential platform that heavily promoted the fair (McGloin, 2005).

Business magnates in various sectors also lent their support. James D. Phelan, a banker and future Mayor of San Francisco, was a member of the Finance Committee for the fair. Phelan's role involved fundraising and ensuring the financial stability of the event, a task crucial for its success given the economic downturn following the Panic of 1893 (Reed, 1989; White, 1993).

One of the critical motivations for the fair was economics.

As mentioned, the United States was grappling with the after-effects of the Panic of 1893, a severe economic depression that had resulted in bank failures, high unemployment, and widespread distress (White, 1993). In this climate, de Young and other civic leaders saw the fair as a means to revitalize the local economy, particularly during the winter months when tourism typically waned (Reed, 1989). Moreover, California's agrarian economy had been affected by the nationwide depression, and the exposition was seen as a platform to showcase the state's agricultural and mineral wealth. The fair was strategically planned to take place during the winter months, offering an inviting climate to potential visitors from colder parts of the country.

Interior of Fine Arts Building, C.M.I.E., 1894

The financial turmoil of 1893 exacerbated underlying economic weaknesses, resulting in several industries' collapse and an estimated unemployment rate of 18% by 1894 (Licht, 1995). Businesses shuttered, leaving thousands of laborers jobless, leading to social unrest. The Pullman Strike of 1894, one of the most significant labor strikes in American history, was a direct consequence of the economic downturn (Papke, 1999).

Another significant motivation was culture. As a relatively young city, San Francisco was keen to establish itself as a cultural and intellectual hub. The exposition provided an opportunity to showcase art, technology, and science advancements, aiming to draw the nation's attention to the city's emerging cultural institutions (Cohen, 2005). In this vein, the Fine Arts Building was created, which would later become the de Young Museum, thus leaving a lasting cultural legacy for the city (Cohen, 2005).

For the fair itself, the architecturally significant structures and exhibitions resulted from collaborations with eminent architects and designers of the era. Arthur Page Brown, known for designing the San Francisco Ferry Building, contributed to the fair by designing the Mechanics Arts Building (Wilson, 2007). His work significantly influenced the architectural aesthetics of the exposition and, subsequently, the city's architectural landscape.

The selection of Golden Gate Park as the venue for the 1894 Midwinter Fair was a strategic decision influenced by various factors. Golden Gate Park, designed by William Hammond Hall and later refined by John McLaren, was one of the most significant urban parks in the United States, providing a verdant landscape in San Francisco (Brechin, 1999). Its spaciousness, natural beauty, and accessibility made it a logical choice for a large-scale event like the Midwinter Fair.

- Firstly, the location was advantageous in terms of logistics. Golden Gate Park offered ample space to house the numerous exhibits, buildings, and attractions planned for the fair (Cohen, 2005). The park's existing infrastructure, including pathways, gardens, and facilities, could be readily adapted for fair purposes, reducing initial setup costs.

- Secondly, the park was strategically situated and easily accessible by the city's burgeoning public transportation network (Hart, 1987). This allowed for convenient entry to and from the fair, catering to residents and tourists. Being a well-known landmark in San Francisco, Golden Gate Park was already a popular destination for leisure activities, which made it an attractive venue for attracting large crowds (Seetharaman, 2008).

- Thirdly, Golden Gate Park symbolized San Francisco's natural beauty and progressive urban planning (Hart, 1987). Hosting the fair in this iconic location was consistent with the event's theme of showcasing California's abundant resources while also demonstrating the city's commitment to public spaces and community well-being.

- Lastly, the choice was influenced by the aspirations of the fair's organizers, notably Michael H. de Young, who envisioned the fair as an event that would elevate San Francisco's standing on the national and international stage (Cohen, 2005). Positioning the Midwinter Fair within Golden Gate Park, a symbol of civic pride and architectural ingenuity, aligned well with de Young's broader objectives of promoting the city and the state during a challenging economic period (Rawls & Bean, 2003).

The construction of the 1894 Midwinter Fair was a remarkable feat, given the timeframe and resources involved. Preparations for the fair began in earnest after its official announcement and it was constructed within a relatively short period, approximately six months, between mid-1893 and January 1894 (Cohen, 2005). We are told this expedited schedule was made possible through a combination of meticulous planning, abundant labor, and the ready availability of construction materials.

Supposedly, the materials for the construction predominantly came from local sources, underscoring the fair's focus on showcasing Californian resources. Timber was sourced from the forests in Northern California, while stone and other masonry materials were quarried from nearby regions (Star & Orsi, 1990). Materials were sometimes recycled from other large-scale projects or events, such as the 1893 Columbian Exposition in Chicago. Items like decorative elements, furnishings, and entire building facades were transported to San Francisco for reuse in the Midwinter Fair (Cohen, 2005). This demonstrated a resourceful use of materials and added an extra layer of connection between the Midwinter Fair and other significant cultural exhibitions of the period.

Labor for the construction was readily available, partly due to the economic downturn caused by the Panic of 1893 (Licht, 1995). The high unemployment rate meant that there was a large pool of laborers eager for work, allowing for the speedy construction of the fair's infrastructure. Both skilled and unskilled workers were employed in various capacities, from carpentry and masonry to landscaping and electrical work. Given the short time frame and the exhibits' complexity, construction proceeded rapidly, often around the clock, to ensure the fair would open on time (Cohen, 2005).

The layout of the 1894 Midwinter Fair was painstakingly planned to accommodate a variety of exhibits, pavilions, and attractions within the expansive space of San Francisco's Golden Gate Park. Architecturally inspired by other grand expositions like the 1893 Columbian Exposition in Chicago, the fairgrounds were designed to captivate visitors with both their scale and diversity (Cohen, 2005).

One of the standout features of the fairgrounds was the grand Court of Honor, which served as the event's focal point. Situated centrally, this space was home to some of the fair's most majestic structures, such as the Fine Arts Building and the Electric Tower (Cohen, 2005). The Court of Honor served as an architectural spectacle and a symbolic center that reflected the fair's ambitions to showcase technological advancement and cultural grandeur (Star & Orsi, 1990).

Multiple avenues lined with international and state exhibits radiated from the Court of Honor. These avenues were thematically organized to guide visitors through a global journey, featuring pavilions from various countries and U.S. states (Hart, 1987). Such a layout facilitated the fair's broader goal of educating the public about different cultures and innovations worldwide. These avenues were typically named after the regions they represented—such as Oriental Avenue, which hosted exhibits from Asia, and State Avenue, home to various U.S. state pavilions (Hart, 1987).

Electric Tower and Grand Court, C.M.I.E., San Francisco

Apart from these, specialty buildings were dispersed throughout the fairgrounds, each dedicated to specific subjects like horticulture, mining, and manufacturing. These specialty buildings offered in-depth exhibitions, often sponsored by industries or governmental organizations keen on demonstrating the wealth of resources and technological innovations particular to their field (Rawls & Bean, 2003).

The fair also featured several entertainment venues, including an amusement area called the Midway Plaisance. Borrowing its name and concept from the 1893 Columbian Exposition, the Midway Plaisance was an eclectic mix of games, rides, and live performances designed to entertain visitors (Seetharaman, 2008). Including such recreational spaces alongside the more educational and cultural exhibits was a strategic move to attract a broader audience, appealing to the intellectually curious and those searching for leisure (Cohen, 2005).

Gardens and natural spaces were interspersed among the buildings and avenues, offering respite from the bustling activities and crowded exhibits. These areas were consistent with Golden Gate Park's identity as an urban oasis and served to highlight San Francisco's natural beauty (Hart, 1987).

Among the specialized areas was the Mechanics Building, where industrial and technological exhibits were showcased. This was an opportunity for the public and industry professionals to witness the cutting-edge innovations of the time (Rawls & Bean, 2003).

Another noteworthy area was the Agricultural Building, dedicated to showcasing California's rich natural resources and farming capabilities. The aim was to exhibit the state's agricultural diversity and potential for economic development in this sector (Star & Orsi, 1990).

The Fine Arts Building was an important feature that displayed many artworks, including paintings, sculptures, and decorative arts. This building aimed to highlight international talents and local artists, thereby positioning San Francisco as a cultural center (Cohen, 2005).

COURT OF HONOR

The Main Buildings, often called the Court of Honor, was the architectural and symbolic epicenter of the 1894 Midwinter Fair in San Francisco's Golden Gate Park. Designed as the fair's grand centerpiece, this area encapsulated the overarching themes and ambitions of the event. One of the most striking features of the Court of Honor was the Electric Tower, a 266-foot-tall structure adorned with thousands of electric lights, which illuminated the fairgrounds at night and served as a beacon of technological prowess (Cohen, 2005).

Another cornerstone structure within the Court of Honor was the Fine Arts Building, later known as the de Young Museum. Named after Michael H. de Young, one of the primary organizers of the fair, this edifice was home to an extensive collection of artworks and was symbolic of the fair's commitment to promoting culture and the arts (Cohen, 2005).

Electric Tower at Night, C.M.I.E., 1894

The Electric Tower and the Fine Arts Building were expressions of the technological and cultural aspirations the fair aimed to project. Their association within the same court emphasized the harmonious blend of technology and culture, a message that resonated with the optimistic visions of the late 19th century (Star & Orsi, 1990).

The Court of Honor was not merely an assemblage of buildings; it also included landscaped gardens, fountains, and sculptures, providing a multi-sensory experience for visitors. These elements were strategically integrated to create a balanced and aesthetically pleasing environment (Hart, 1987).

Court of Honor, 1894

The use of classical architectural styles in the Court of Honor, inspired by Greco-Roman motifs, intentionally linked the fair to a broader historical and cultural lineage. This choice also aligned with the Beaux-Arts architectural trends of the era, which were prevalent in other grand expositions, including the 1893 Columbian Exposition in Chicago (Seetharaman, 2008).

Overall, the Court of Honor physically manifested the fair's ideals and aspirations. Its architectural elements, the variety of exhibits it housed, and its stylistic influences combined to create a visually stunning and intellectually stimulating environment. The Court was a focal point where technological innovation met artistic expression, capturing the spirit of an age keen on heralding a new era of progress and cultural enlightenment.

FINE ARTS BUILDING

The Fine Arts Building, which later evolved into the de Young Museum, held a role of paramount importance in the 1894 Midwinter Fair. Positioned within the Court of Honor, the building was not merely an enclosure for artworks but a symbol of the cultural aspirations and achievements that the fair sought to epitomize. The inclusion of the Fine Arts Building signaled an earnest attempt to elevate public taste and underscore the intellectual merit of the event (Cohen, 2005).

Original Sphinx, Fine Arts Building, 1894

Named after Michael H. de Young, as mentioned, one of the primary organizers of the fair and co-founder of the "San Francisco Chronicle," the building showcased an array of artistic mediums, including painting, sculpture, and decorative arts (Cohen, 2005). By presenting both international and domestic works, the organizers sought to place San Francisco on the global cultural map. This aspiration was particularly significant in a burgeoning city aiming to establish itself as a metropolis with economic and cultural capital (Star & Orsi, 1990).

The collection within the Fine Arts Building was carefully curated to appeal to a wide range of visitors, from casual spectators to serious art aficionados. This strategy was aligned with the broader educational mission of the fair, which aimed to serve as a locus of public enlightenment and cultural edification (Hart, 1987).

Moreover, the architectural design of the Fine Arts Building itself was an exhibit of grandeur. Adhering to the Beaux-Arts style, which was prevalent in late 19th-century public buildings, the structure combined classical elements with modern building techniques. This architectural choice can be seen as reflective of the era's broader fascination with a harmonious blend of tradition and innovation, a theme that was prevalent in other grand expositions of the time, such as the 1893 Columbian Exposition in Chicago (Seetharaman, 2008).

COPYRIGHT BY I.W. TABER 1894

8055 The Fine Arts Building, California Midwinter International Exposition, 1894.

Fine Arts Building during Midwinter Fair, 1894

Post-fair, the Fine Arts Building transitioned into the de Young Museum, securing its legacy as a cornerstone of San Francisco's cultural landscape. This transformation ensured that the building would continue to serve as an institution for public education and cultural enrichment long after the Midwinter Fair's conclusion (Cohen, 2005).

In summary, the Fine Arts Building (later the de Young Museum) was not merely a venue for displaying artworks but served as a critical component of the Midwinter Fair's intellectual and cultural agenda. Its role was to offer a sophisticated environment that fostered artistic appreciation and education, thereby contributing to the fair's broader mission of elevating public style and promoting San Francisco as a rising center of culture and learning.

MECHANICAL ARTS BUILDING

The Mechanical Arts Building was another significant edifice within the 1894 Midwinter Fair's architectural landscape. Situated in a prominent fairground location, this building was designed to embody industrial progress and technological innovation (Cohen, 2005). Like its counterpart, the Fine Arts Building, the Mechanical Arts Building aimed to serve educational and entertainment purposes.

Mechanical Arts Building on right, 1894

The structure of the Mechanical Arts Building was in keeping with the overarching Beaux-Arts architectural style of the fair, which blended classical design elements with modern construction techniques. The building was an amalgamation of materials such as steel, glass, and wood, showcasing the engineering capabilities it was designed to celebrate (Seetharaman, 2008).

Inside, the Mechanical Arts Building housed various exhibits demonstrating machinery, engineering, and technological advances. The displays, from intricate textile looms to steam engines, underscored America's industrial prowess. The layout was meticulously designed to guide visitors through a narrative of human ingenuity, starting with simpler mechanical devices and progressing toward more complex machines and inventions (Cohen, 2005).

One of the key attractions within the Mechanical Arts Building was the Electricity Pavilion, which housed cutting-edge electrical devices and machinery of the era (Cohen, 2005). The emphasis on electrical technologies was no accident; it reflected the period's fascination with electricity as a harbinger of future possibilities, and such an exhibit served as a powerful statement on the transformative potential of technology and its capacity to shape the future (Star & Orsi, 1990).

8332   Mechanic Arts Building, California Midwinter International Exposition. 1894.   Copyright 1894, by Taber Photo.

Mechanical Arts Building, 1894

In an era marked by rapid industrialization and significant technological advancement, the Mechanical Arts Building allowed visitors to witness the marvels of human invention firsthand. The building served as a tangible manifestation of the United States' aspirations to be seen as a leader in technological innovation, mirroring similar aspirations evident in earlier expositions such as the 1893 Columbian Exposition in Chicago (Seetharaman, 2008).

In summary, the Mechanical Arts Building played a critical role in the Midwinter Fair's endeavor to illustrate the wonders of American industry and technological progress. Its architectural design, exhibit layout, and various machinery on display were all crafted to create an environment where industrial achievement could be appreciated, understood, and celebrated. In doing so, the building reinforced the fair's more prominent theme of progress and possibility, contributing significantly to its overall impact and legacy.

HORTICULTURAL HALL

Allegorical Fountain and Agricultural Building, C.M.I.E., 1894

The Horticultural Hall at the 1894 Midwinter Fair in San Francisco held a unique and specialized role in the fair's grand design. This building was mainly dedicated to displaying and celebrating plants, flowers, and various other forms of vegetation, emphasizing the importance of horticulture both as a science and an art form (Cohen, 2005). It served as an educational space, offering the general populace an opportunity to become acquainted with diverse plant species, some of which were exotic and not native to the United States (Star & Orsi, 1990).

Architecturally, the Horticultural Hall was designed to harmonize with its contents. It often included elements that mimicked natural forms, thus creating an aesthetically pleasing environment that enhanced the presentation of the plant species inside (Seetharaman, 2008). The building was generally spacious, allowing for arranging plants and flowers in an elaborate yet accessible manner. In keeping with the rest of the fair, its architectural style was influenced by the prevalent Beaux-Arts style, though adapted to suit the specific needs of a greenhouse-like structure (Hart, 1987).

Horticulture and Agriculture Building, night

Within Horticultural Hall, visitors could expect to find a variety of displays ranging from ornamental plants and flowers to exhibits focusing on agricultural productivity. One could encounter a multitude of flora, including orchids, roses, ferns, and fruits and vegetables, showcasing California's fertility and agricultural richness (Cohen, 2005). These exhibits were often sponsored or created in collaboration with local and regional horticultural societies, agricultural colleges, and individual growers (Rawls & Bean, 2003).

The hall was not solely a place for passive observation; it often hosted lectures and demonstrations to disseminate knowledge about best practices in horticulture. These sessions would cover various topics like plant breeding, soil management, and the role of horticulture in broader ecological systems (Seetharaman, 2008).

The Horticultural Hall's significance also extended to its post-fair legacy. Like the Fine Arts Building that became the de Young Museum, the Horticultural Hall also served as a foundation for later botanical research and education in the region (Cohen, 2005).

In summary, Horticultural Hall was not merely an ancillary feature of the 1894 Midwinter Fair but was an integral part of its educational and cultural mission. By featuring various plant species and hosting educational sessions, the hall underscored the importance of horticulture in the broader social and economic landscape of the time, contributing to the fair's overall aims of education and enlightenment.

ADMINISTRATIVE BUILDINGS AND SMALLER STRUCTURES

The administrative buildings and smaller structures at the 1894 Midwinter Fair were integral to the operational and logistical framework of the event. These buildings were meticulously designed to serve specific functions, including the administration of fair activities, ticketing, and information dissemination, among other roles (Cohen, 2005).

Administrative Building & Garden, 1894

In terms of architectural design, these structures were generally more straightforward than the more significant thematic buildings like the Mechanical Arts Building or Fine Arts Building. Nevertheless, they adhered to the fair's overall Beaux-

Arts aesthetic, which combined classical design principles with elements of modernity (Seetharaman, 2008). Although not as grand as some of the thematic pavilions, the administrative buildings were equally crucial for the fair's overall success.

Fountain, 1894

One of the key administrative buildings was the Fair's Headquarters, which served as the nerve center for the entire exposition. It was typically where major decisions concerning the event's management were made and where organizers, including figures like Michael H. de Young, coordinated their activities (Cohen, 2005). This building was essential for the centralized management of an event of this magnitude, which included exhibitions and many social activities, performances, and educational programs (Star & Orsi, 1990).

Another noteworthy structure was the Information Center, designed to guide visitors through the extensive fairgrounds. At a time when the concept of information design was still nascent, the Information Center played a crucial role in enhancing the visitor experience, offering maps, schedules, and details about various exhibits and attractions (Rawls & Bean, 2003).

In addition to these, there were also minor structures like restrooms, first aid stations, and lost-and-found centers, all designed to cater to the basic needs of the visitors. Although often overlooked in the grand scheme of things, these smaller structures contributed significantly to the convenience and overall experience of those attending the fair (Hart, 1987).

In summary, while the administrative buildings and smaller structures may not have been the most eye-catching elements of the 1894 Midwinter Fair, they were indispensable for its smooth functioning. Serving various logistical and operational needs, these constructions played a crucial role in enhancing the visitor's enjoyment and contributing significantly to the fair's overall success.

CONTRIBUTIONS

The 1894 Midwinter Fair in San Francisco served as a platform for exhibiting various technological advancements, particularly in the Mechanical Arts Building, which was a locus for showcasing innovation. The fair came at the cusp of a new century, during a period when the United States was transitioning into a modern industrialized nation (Star & Orsi, 1990). Several groundbreaking technologies were displayed, highlighting the nation's advances in mechanical engineering, electricity, transportation, and telecommunications.

One of the most notable exhibits was that of electrical technologies. Following closely on the heels of the 1893 Columbian Exposition in Chicago, where Nikola Tesla and George Westinghouse had introduced the public to alternating current (AC), the 1894 Midwinter Fair also showcased advancements in electrical power and lighting (Cohen, 2005). Electrical arc lights and incandescent bulbs were prominently displayed, providing an insight into how electricity was poised to revolutionize domestic life and industrial work (Seetharaman, 2008).

Automobiles were another significant technological innovation presented at the fair. Although still in their infancy and not yet a common sight, early versions of motor vehicles were exhibited to demonstrate their potential for personal and commercial transportation (Hart, 1987). The display captured the public's imagination, presenting a future where engine-powered vehicles would replace horse-drawn carriages (Rawls & Bean, 2003).

Telecommunications also featured prominently, with exhibits on telegraphy and the nascent field of telephony. These technologies were seen as critical for the nation's development, offering faster and more efficient methods of communication over long distances (Seetharaman, 2008).

Additionally, the fair showcased a range of domestic appliances aimed at reducing household labor and improving the quality of home life. From early washing machines to rudimentary vacuum cleaners, these exhibits emphasized the role technology was expected to play in freeing up leisure time and standardizing domestic chores (Cohen, 2005).

Italian Exhibits, in Manufacturers' Building, C.M.I.E.

The fair also highlighted advances in agriculture through mechanized farming equipment. Plows, harvesters, and other machinery were displayed, representing the modernization of farming practices and the drive toward greater agricultural efficiency (Star & Orsi, 1990).

In summary, the 1894 Midwinter Fair offered a window into a future shaped by technological advancements. The exhibits covered a broad spectrum of innovation—from electrical engineering to domestic appliances—each contributing to the chronicle of American progress and modernity at the turn of the century. By showcasing these innovations, the fair entertained its visitors and educated them on the transformative power of technology in shaping the twentieth century.

The Fine Arts Building showcased many artworks, ranging from paintings and sculptures to textiles and decorative arts. These displays were designed to offer visitors an educational experience, exposing them to various art forms and artistic styles. Works by European masters were exhibited alongside those by emerging American artists, providing a broad scope of artistic expression (Rawls & Bean, 2003).

One of the major highlights was the collection of European paintings, which included masterpieces from the Renaissance to the modern era. This section was instrumental in familiarizing the American public with European art traditions and standards, thereby serving as a form of cultural education (Hart, 1987).

The inclusion of American artists was a significant feature of the Fine Arts Building, contributing to the narrative of a burgeoning national artistic identity. The fair organizers made a compelling statement about the country's evolving cultural landscape by placing American art in the same space as European art. The exhibit helped spotlight the works of local Californian artists as well, thus giving them a platform to gain recognition (Seetharaman, 2008).

Moreover, the Fine Arts Building hosted a series of thematic exhibitions aimed at exploring various art forms and their cultural contexts. These included exhibits dedicated to Asian and Native American art, thereby acknowledging the diversity of cultural influences shaping American art and society. Such displays were relatively novel at the time and represented a significant endeavor to diversify the artistic representation at the fair (Star & Orsi, 1990).

In addition to traditional art forms, the Fine Arts Building also featured innovative displays like dioramas, artistic photography, and other mixed-media installations, embracing newer forms of artistic expression (Cohen, 2005).

The 1894 Midwinter Fair served as a stage for various exhibitors to showcase many products, inventions, and talents. The exhibitors ranged from industrial moguls to inventors and artisans. They hailed from different parts of the United States and worldwide, making the event an international platform for exhibiting innovation, craftsmanship, and cultural exchange.

One of the most significant exhibitors was Edison General Electric, a company founded by the famed inventor Thomas Edison. The company displayed a variety of electrical devices and innovations, offering a glimpse into the future of electricity as a transformative societal force (Hughes, 1989). This participation by Edison General Electric marked an important milestone in the public understanding and acceptance of electrical technology.

Similarly, the Southern Pacific Railroad had an extensive exhibit that focused on the development of the railroad industry and its economic impact on the Western United States. The exhibit highlighted technological innovations in rail transport and emphasized the railroad's role in facilitating commerce and connecting disparate geographical regions (Ambrose, 2000).

In the realm of consumer goods, companies like Procter & Gamble showcased their household products, aiming to captivate the domestic market. Demonstrations of the efficacy and benefits of these products offered visitors practical insights into their daily lives, thus serving as an early form of consumer education (Friedel, 2007).

Various states and countries also set up pavilions to showcase their culture, industry, and natural resources. For instance, the Japanese pavilion featured traditional crafts, tea ceremonies, and cultural performances, providing a window into Japanese culture and aesthetics (Ishizuka, 2006). These national pavilions were crucial in broadening the public's knowledge and appreciation of global cultures and products.

In the agricultural sector, companies and organizations presented new farming techniques and machinery, illustrating advancements in agriculture and their potential to improve food production and security (Danbom, 1995).

Additionally, academic institutions participated in the fair, highlighting ongoing research and advancements in various scientific disciplines. These exhibits often included intricate models, interactive displays, and lectures to educate the public about scientific progress (Kohlstedt, 1994).

To conclude the narrative we are given, the 1894 Midwinter Fair was a diverse congregation of exhibitors presenting various technological innovations, cultural artifacts, and commercial products. The fair catalyzed numerous industries and academic disciplines, providing them with a platform to engage with the public and share their contributions to society.

Approximately 2.2 million people attended the fair, a remarkable number considering the population of the United States at the time (Harland, 1894). This figure underlines the magnitude and appeal of the event, especially given the prevailing economic conditions following the Panic of 1893.

In terms of demographics, the fair attracted a diverse array of visitors. Local San Franciscans comprised a considerable portion of the attendees, but people from various parts of California and the broader United States were also well-represented (Harland, 1894; Pryor, 1895). The fair's extensive marketing campaigns targeted middle-class families, emphasizing educational value and wholesome entertainment as key attractions (Cross & Walton, 2005). As a result, families with children constituted a significant demographic, aligning with the fair's aim to offer an educational experience.

Furthermore, the fair had a robust attendance from professionals and entrepreneurs, particularly those engaged in industries that were featured prominently in the exhibitions. These included engineers, inventors, artists, and academic representatives (Smith, 2007). Their presence signified the fair's relevance and impact on various professional domains.

Interestingly, the fair also attracted international visitors, which included diplomats, foreign journalists, and tourists. The international pavilions and exhibits from various countries drew a global audience, thus adding an international dimension to the event (Badger, 1989).

Overall, the 1894 Midwinter Fair was a significant event in terms of public reception, attracting a broad cross-section of society. While it primarily catered to middle-class American families, the fair offered something for people of diverse backgrounds, professions, and interests. It had supposed success in drawing a large and varied audience, exemplifying its universal appeal and underscoring its impact as a cultural and technological landmark.

Vintage Illustration of Midwinter Exposition, 1894

CHAPTER 8: THE WIZARD OF NOPE
DECONSTRUCTING THE 1894 NARRATIVE

IDENTIFYING IMPOSSIBLE NARRATIVES

Focusing on the 1894 Midwinter Fair, a significant part of the fair's infrastructure was the Boiler Annex, located behind the Mechanical Building. This facility featured two smokestacks and, if the narrative were true, would have functioned as the main electrical generator for the fair. It would have used coal as fuel to generate Direct Current (DC) electricity. In 1894, the average wholesale price for a ton of mid-grade coal in the United States was approximately $0.95 (U.S. Bureau of Labor Statistics, 1895). The cost was determined by various factors such as the quality of the coal, location, and available supply routes. While this might seem relatively low by today's standards, it is worth noting that $0.95 in 1894 would be roughly equivalent to about $35 in 2023 when adjusted for inflation (CPI et al., 2023).

The first power plant in California was the Folsom Powerhouse, located in Folsom, California, roughly 100 miles east of San Francisco's Golden Gate Park as the crow flies (in a straight line). It commenced operations on July 13, 1895. This is a year and a half too late for our 1894 event, not that it could have provided electricity over that distance during that time, but since it was not constructed yet, there is no need to address that argument.

It is worth noting that this Folsom hydroelectric facility was groundbreaking in several ways, including its use of alternating current (AC). While AC allowed further transmission differences, we still talk in tens of miles in 1894, not hundreds. The plant generated electricity by harnessing the power of the American River, and the electricity produced was initially used to power Sacramento's streetcars and lights, about 22 miles from the powerhouse (Hundt, 1997).

Smokestacks behind Mechanical Building, 1984

Coal was the dominant electrical generation fuel during this period, offering reliable and stable energy output (Williams, 1998). The choice of DC electrical systems was strategic because DC is efficient for short-distance power distribution (Hughes, 1983).

Thomas Edison, a strong proponent of DC systems, was an exhibitor at the fair (Hughes, 1989). As already noted, he displayed various electrical technologies, contributing to the fair's focus on technological innovation. The Boiler Annex would have served not only as functional infrastructure but also as a large-scale demonstration of the viability and advantages of DC power systems. Its operation would resonate with Edison's ongoing campaign to establish DC as the dominant electrical standard.

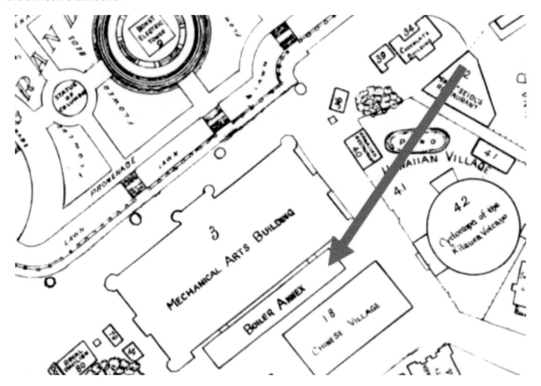

Boiler Annex on 1894 Diagram

For all this to work, the dedicated coal-fired power plant known as the Boiler Annex was centrally located behind the Mechanical Arts Building. The use of coal as the primary fuel for the plant would be consistent with the energy landscape of the late 19th century, where coal-fired plants were the mainstay of electricity generation (Hughes, 1983).

The direct current system, however, came with its set of challenges, primarily the issue of distance-related inefficiencies in transmission. Transmission lines made of heavy-duty electrical cables would be the arterial routes connecting the Boiler Annex to the sprawling exhibition site. This network would include a comprehensive assembly of switchgear and control panels designed to regulate electricity distribution throughout the venue. These control mechanisms would be indispensable in demarcating electrical zones and managing specific features, such as lighting (Hughes, 1983).

An elaborate network of low-voltage electrical wiring would be necessary for the illumination component to connect the multitude of light bulbs spread across the venue. The fixtures housing these bulbs would vary from decorative to utilitarian, determined by both aesthetic preferences and safety regulations of the exposition. Outdoor lighting would require its own dedicated infrastructure, including poles, fixtures, and wiring, and would likely operate on a separate circuit to avoid compromising system reliability.

1894 Midwinter at Night

Critical to the successful functioning of this electrical system would be the accurate calculation of the total electrical load, considering all the components that would draw power, from lighting fixtures to machinery. Load calculations would be the cornerstone for engineering a robust and reliable system that meets the exposition's demands (Hughes, 1983). Methods for load balancing would also be instituted, ensuring that the system could efficiently handle variations in power demand, particularly during periods of high electrical consumption, such as nighttime.

It is not easy to precisely quantify the level of electrical power that would have been needed. The essential components of the DC system would have been power generation, transmission, substation boost, distribution, and then an electrical piece of equipment like a light bulb, machine, or motor at the end of the run. Even by conservative estimates, the power requirements would be significant—likely on the order of several hundred kilowatts to perhaps a few megawatts, depending on the specifics of the lighting and other electrical needs (Nye, 1990). We will assume one megawatt for our analysis as that volume is the middle of the possible scale, and we can see the massive lighting effects in photographs.

Calculating the amount of coal needed to power an event like the 1894 California Midwinter International Exposition for a duration of six months is a complex task. The calculations would depend on multiple factors, such as electrical demand, the efficiency of steam boilers and generators, and the time for which electrical power is required each day. Due to the absence of accurate data concerning these variables, it is essential to note that any resultant calculation will be an approximation.

To frame a theoretical model, it is helpful to consider that steam engines in the late 19th century had efficiencies ranging from 2% to 10% (Rosenberg, 1982). The energy density of coal, another critical parameter, varies approximately between 24 and 35 MJ/kg (World Coal Association, 2023). For this illustration, let us use medium-grade coal with an energy density of 30 MJ/kg.

If the fair required a steady power output of 1 Megawatt (MW) each day, the daily power usage would be calculated as 1 MW multiplied by 24 hours daily, resulting in 24 Megawatt-hours per day. In equation form, this can be represented as:

$$1MW * 24 \ hours/day = 24 \ MWh/day$$

When converting this to Megajoules, we find:

$$24 \ MWh/day * 3.6 * 10^6 \ J/MWh = 8.64 * 10^7 \ MJ/day$$

Considering a 5% efficiency of the average boiler and generator, the amount of input energy from coal needed would be:

$$8.64 * 10^7 \ MJ/day / 0.05 = 1.728 * 10^9 \ MJ/day$$

Given that the selected medium-grade coal has an energy density of 30 MJ/kg, the daily coal requirement can be calculated as follows:

$$1.728 * 10^9 \ MJ/day / 30 \ MJ/kg = 5.76 * 10^7 \ kg/day$$

Or, in other terms, 57,600 metric tons per day.

For a time frame of approximately 180 days or six months, the total coal requirement would be:

$$57,600 \ metric \ tons/day * 180 \ days = 10,368,000 \ metric \ tons$$

1894 Midwinter at Night Agriculture Building

Under these conditions, it can be approximated that around 10.4 million metric tons of coal would be needed to sustain the fair's electrical systems for six months. We need to convert this to pounds and tons to calculate the cost. The daily coal requirement in our scenario was calculated as 57,600 metric tons per day. Converting this to pounds:

*57,600 metric tons/day * 2204.62 pounds/metric ton = $1.27 * 10^8$ pounds/day*

For the six-month duration or approximately 180 days, the total coal requirement would be:

*$1.27 * 10^8$ pounds/day * 180 days = $2.286 * 10^{10}$ pounds*

Now, let us turn our attention to the cost aspect. Historical records suggest that the price of mid-grade coal in 1894 was around $0.95 per ton (Aldrich, 1997). Converting this to the cost per pound would yield:

$0.95 /metric ton / 2204.62 pounds/metric ton = $4.31 * 10^{-4}$ /pound

Thus, the daily cost of coal would be:

$$1.27 * 10^8 \text{ pounds/day} * \$4.31 * 10^{-4} \text{/pound} = \$54,837 \text{/day}$$

For the six-month duration, the total cost would be:

$$\$54,837 \text{/day} * 180 \text{ days} = \$9,870,660$$

Under these assumptions, the estimated budget for the coal needed to run the electrical systems of the 1894 California Midwinter International Exposition for six months would be approximately $9.87 million in 1894 dollars.

However, we still have to get the coal to the fair. To compute the number of train cars required daily to transport the calculated volume of coal, several parameters need to be defined: the carrying capacity of a single train car and the daily requirement of coal in pounds. In the late 19th century, a standard train car could hold about 50 tons (or 100,000 pounds) of coal (Solomon, 2001).

Manufacturers Building & Fountain, Night, 1894

In our prior calculations, the daily coal requirement was 1.27×10^8 pounds. Dividing this by the carrying capacity of one train car gives:

$$(1.27 \times 10^8 \; pounds/day) / 100,000 \; pounds/train \; car = 1270 \; train \; cars/day$$

Therefore, under these assumptions, approximately 1,270 train cars would be needed daily to meet the daily coal requirement for powering the electrical systems at the 1894 California Midwinter International Exposition. We would pile on and now calculate the labor costs required to load and unload 1,270 train cars a day, each full of 100,000 pounds of coal, but we will leave that to your imagination.

Instead, let us now consider the cost of transporting the coal via train. The cost of transporting coal by rail in the late 19th century varied depending on several factors, such as distance, rail tariffs, and the contractual arrangements between coal suppliers and railroads. However, for the purpose of this estimation, let us consider a historical average cost of around 2 cents per ton-mile (Fishlow, 1965).

To transport 57,600 metric tons of coal daily (equivalent to 1.27×10^8 pounds), we must multiply the weight by the cost per ton-mile and then by the distance the coal needs to be transported. The distance would vary depending on the source of the coal and could range anywhere from a few miles to several hundred miles. For the sake of this discussion, let us assume a distance of 100 miles, which would include Oakland, Sacramento, and enough geography for reasonable coal production:

$$2 \; cents/ton\text{-}mile * 57,600 \; metric \; tons * 100 \; miles = \$115,200/day$$

Translating this into a six-month operation (or approximately 180 days) yields:

$$\$115,200/day * 180 \; days = \$20,736,000$$

Under these assumptions, the total cost of transporting the coal required to power the electrical systems of the exposition for six months would be around $20.74 million. Adding this to our previously calculated coal purchase cost of $9.87 million, the combined expense would amount to:

$$\$20,736,000 \; (transport) + \$9,870,660 \; (coal) = \$30,606,660$$

Therefore, it can be estimated that approximately $30.6 million would be the combined cost of purchasing and transporting the coal for six months, given the assumptions and historical pricing.

So, this is great; we have built a boiler annex and have enough coal. Now we have to get the power out into the fair's 200 acres and 120 buildings, with five large central buildings—including the Mechanical Building—two electric fountains, and a 266-foot-tall central tower adorned with lights and a rotating searchlight. The electrical wiring for these structures was differently configured: the central buildings and the tower had their wiring buried underground, while the smaller, peripheral buildings were served by overhead wires supported on poles. This complexity warrants a comprehensive estimation of the amount and cost of the required wiring and the labor and logistics involved in the installation.

The smaller outlying buildings likely required between 50 to 100 feet of wiring. With 115 such structures, taking an average of 75 feet per building, the wiring for these would total approximately 8,625 feet.

Since the Mechanical Building was one of the five major central structures, it would have more complex electrical needs, possibly requiring around 10,000 feet of wiring.

We might estimate an average of 5,000 feet of wiring each for the remaining four central buildings and the electric fountains. This would total 30,000 feet for these six installations.

The 266-foot tower would also require a considerable amount of wiring, approximately 10,000 feet, to support its complex lighting and rotating searchlight.

Summing up, the entire fair would have needed:

8,625 feet (smaller buildings) + 10,000 feet (Mechanical Building) + 30,000 feet (other central installations) + 10,000 feet (266-foot tower) = 58,625 feet

The cost of copper wiring in 1894 was around $0.50 per pound (U.S. Geological Survey, 1894). Using the approximation that one mile of copper wire weighs about 5,000 pounds (Griffiths, 2012), the weight of the total wiring would be approximately 55,590 pounds.

The corresponding financial expenditure would be:

$$55,590 \text{ pounds} \times \$0.50/pound = \$27,795$$

Installing the wiring would have involved challenges and costs for above-ground and underground installations. For the former, poles would need to be erected. A single wooden utility pole in the 1890s might cost around $10 (including labor), and we might estimate one pole per 150 feet of wire, requiring approximately 58 poles for the smaller buildings (Smith, 1896). This would sum up to $580 for the pole installations.

For the underground installations, labor would be more intensive. Trenching, laying conduit, and burying the cable could cost around $2 per foot in 1894 (Smith, 1896). For the 50,000 feet of wiring for the central structures and the tower, this would amount to $100,000.

Considering the extensive range of electrical installations required for the exposition—from the smaller outlying structures to the central complexes—a total of approximately 58,625 feet of wiring would be needed. The estimated cost for the copper wiring would be about $27,795. Labor and logistics costs would significantly add to this, with $580 for pole installations and $100,000 for underground installations. Therefore, the estimated wiring and installation budget would be around $128,375.

Electrical Tower at Night

We have already exhausted the proposed budget of $1.1M fifty times over, and we have not constructed a single building. Unfortunately, just getting this electrical grid installed exhausts the timeline for the fair as well. In addition to the financial costs and labor requirements, understanding the time needed for such an endeavor provides a crucial context for its implementation. The timeline for wiring the 1894 California Midwinter International Exposition would be influenced by several critical factors, including material procurement, labor availability, and the specific steps involved in above ground and underground installations.

The lead time for acquiring 58,625 feet of copper wiring, along with the necessary insulating and conduit materials, might reasonably be estimated at one month. This estimate is contingent on the state of the industry at the time and assumes that there were no significant supply chain issues (Beauchamp, 1901).

The workforce for such a project would have consisted of skilled and semi-skilled laborers. The labor requirement can be estimated by breaking down the project into its major components:

- **Utility Poles for Above-ground Wiring**: With a team of five laborers, installing 58 poles could likely be accomplished in 2-3 weeks. Each pole could be erected and secured in a day, and multiple poles could be worked on concurrently (Smith, 1896).

- **Trenching for Underground Wiring**: Given that the central buildings and the tower needed 50,000 feet of underground wiring, and if a team of ten workers could achieve about 1,000 feet of trenched and prepared ground per week, this process would take about 4-6 weeks (Smith, 1896).

- **Wiring Installation**: Once the poles are up and the trenches are prepared, installing the actual wires would commence. This could overlap with the trenching stage, allowing for the above-ground and underground wiring to be installed concurrently. Again, a reasonable estimate for this stage would be 4-6 weeks, with a larger team of perhaps 20 electricians (Smith, 1896).

- **Testing and Safety Checks**: The final stage would involve comprehensive testing of all electrical installations to ensure safety and functionality. This would likely take an additional 1-2 weeks (Smith, 1896).

Considering the estimated timelines for each component of the project—material procurement (1 month), utility pole erection (2-3 weeks), trenching (4-6 weeks), wiring installation (4-6 weeks), and safety checks (1-2 weeks)—the entire electrical installation could be reasonably expected to be completed in approximately 4 to 5 months. This hypothetical schedule does not account for delays such as inclement weather, labor strikes, or other unforeseen logistical challenges.

PLUMBING

While not the deal-breaker that electricity was for the budget, plumbing presents a logistical problem for the construction timeline we are given. The fair held its groundbreaking ceremony on August 24, 1893, and opened on January 27, 1894.

That is 157 days.

We have images of the supposed grading and scraping of the fairgrounds that started the same day as the groundbreaking. As you can see in the below image, fourteen carts and maybe fifty horses are present. The scene is hopeless; the men in that image are not grading or scraping anything, yet we are meant to believe that all this work was completed sometime early in the 157 days such that foundation work could start, and then the fair buildings could be built.

Grading work for the 1894 Fair

The late 19th century represented a pivotal moment in public health and civil engineering history. The year 1894 found societies at the cusp of modernity, grappling with the opportunities and challenges of industrialization. One of the significant areas of focus was plumbing, as burgeoning urban centers required increasingly sophisticated water supply and waste management systems. While the basic principles of plumbing had been understood for some time, the technological advancements of this period enabled more complex and reliable systems to be built, especially for large public gatherings and events. Against this backdrop, the 1894 California Midwinter International Exposition was conceived, requiring a complex plumbing infrastructure to accommodate its projected 2.2 million visitors.

Manmade Lake, 1894

In terms of material costs, iron piping was commonly used for plumbing infrastructure in the late 19th century. Historical records suggest the cost per foot of iron piping was approximately $0.25 in 1894 (Flinn, 1895). For simplicity, let us assume that 50,000 feet of iron piping are required. The formula for the material cost would be:

$$50,000 * 0.25 = \$12,500$$

Labor is another crucial consideration. According to records from the U.S. Bureau of Labor Statistics for the period, skilled craftsmen earned around $2 per day (U.S. Bureau of Labor Statistics, 1895). If we assume that at least 100 workers are needed for 90 days, the formula for labor cost would be:

$$100 * 90 * 2 = \$18,000$$

Specialized features such as fountains and fire safety systems would necessitate additional plumbing, thereby increasing the costs. An additional sum of approximately $10,000 might be reasonable for these requirements.

Therefore, summing up these costs, the total estimated expenditure for the plumbing infrastructure would be:

$$\$12,500 \ (Materials) + \$18,000 \ (Labor) + \$10,000 \ (Specialized \ Requirements) = \$40,500$$

Regarding the timeline, an initial planning phase of 2-3 months would be necessary for activities like detailed engineering assessments, procurement planning, and labor arrangements. Subsequently, the construction phase would last approximately 4-5 months, depending on factors such as workforce size, weather conditions, and logistical intricacies. An additional month would be necessary to test the systems and adjust. Thus, the entire project, from the planning stage to commissioning, could span roughly 7-9 months.

While these numbers are simplified approximations, they highlight the magnitude and complexity of implementing such a large-scale plumbing infrastructure in 1894 (Jackson, 2006; Flinn, 1895; U.S. Bureau of Labor Statistics, 1895). The challenge is that even with all this plumbing infrastructure built, we still need water and a reservoir. The narrative is that the Strawberry Hill Sweeny Observatory, constructed in 1891, was converted into a cistern and reservoir that fed the large man-made lake seen in images by the 1894 fair.

Golden Gate Park. Strawberry Hill, Huntington Falls, Sweeny Observatory

In the late 19th century, the engineering and construction techniques for creating lakes, cisterns, and water features were considerably labor-intensive, given the absence of today's heavy machinery (Peterson, 2002). Excavating a lake, digging a cistern, and engineering a waterfall required a sizable workforce and a significant span of time.

For example, digging the lake would have necessitated not just the removal of the earth but also the preparation of the basin to prevent seepage. This phase, which could have taken several months to complete, required substantial manual labor using basic tools such as shovels, pickaxes, and horse-drawn carts (Casson, 1998).

To prevent leakage, the construction of the cistern required durable materials and specialized labor, such as stonemasons and engineers, who would work for weeks on the project. The cistern could have been built using brick or stone lined with an impermeable material (Billington et al., 2005).

Moreover, constructing the waterfall would necessitate both aesthetic and functional considerations. For instance, a system would be required to regulate the water flow from the cistern to the waterfall and, ultimately, the lake. Given that the waterfall was approximately 50 feet above the lake and 35 feet below the hill's peak, the construction process would add a layer of complexity and require specialized engineering and labor. This phase might require a few additional months (Hager, 2009).

Considering the timeline for all these tasks, unexpected variables such as inclement weather, labor shortages, and unforeseen engineering challenges could prolong the project (Kranakis, 1997). Therefore, a conservative estimate for completing the entire project in the socio-technical context of 1894 might fall within one to one and a half years.

Lake below Strawberry Hill, 1894

To better represent the electrical and plumbing scope, the below image from the San Francisco Memories website shows a drawing of the fair's layout and an index. This is the same image used previously to show the Boiler Annex. The shaded section is where all the electrical wiring and plumbing were buried. Everything outside the shaded section had above-ground electrical wiring on poles and had limited plumbing.

Also, note that the quality of the structures is vastly different inside the shaded area and outside. Inside the area, the buildings are majestic and advanced; outside the shaded area, the buildings are rudimentary and very temporary in presentation.

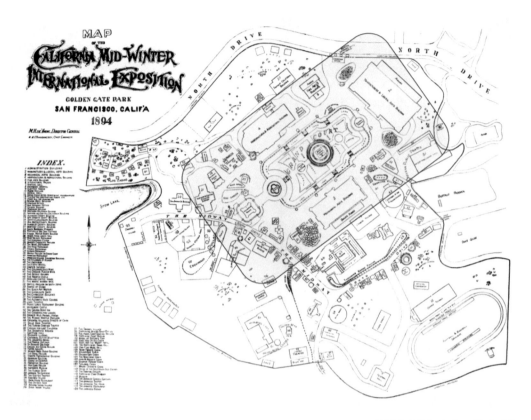

1894 Midwinter Fair Map

OTHER ODDITIES OF THE 1894 MIDWINTER FAIR

The 1894 California Midwinter International Exposition in San Francisco has several odd features and inconsistencies that call for closer examination. Among these are missing images of the Boiler Annex in some photographs, unidentified electrical elements in the Court of Honor, Arthur Page Brown's concurrent architectural projects, and dating issues in the Examiner newspaper. These irregularities compelled us to probe deeper into the event's planning and management.

Firstly, the Boiler Annex, a crucial part of the fair's setup, is notably absent in some photographs. Given the deliberate nature of photography at the time, this absence invites questions about the Annex's significance within the fair (Rosenblum, 1989).

Secondly, unexplained electrical devices are visible in the Court of Honor photographs. These appear to be wired, suggesting a functional role. This raises questions about the technological experiments that might have been underway during the event (Hughes, 1983).

Thirdly, a prominent architect of the fair, Arthur Page Brown, known for his architectural designs, was committed to simultaneously designing the San Francisco Ferry Building, the most immense construction undertaking to date in San Francisco. This creates a puzzle—how was he simultaneously involved in two large projects (Hitchcock, 1977)?

Finally, a groundbreaking discovery on our part after hours of meticulous scouring of historical records. We found a discrepancy in the San Francisco Examiner newspaper's dating of the fair's opening, which adds another layer of complexity. The paper's timeline conflicts with known planning dates by over a year, leading us to question the event's organization and promotion (Schlereth, 1987).

BOILER ANNEX

The Boiler Annex at the 1894 California Midwinter International Exposition poses a perplexing issue due to its inconsistent appearance in archival photographs. Its absence in some archival photographs becomes even more puzzling, considering the time and effort that went into photography during this period. Photography was neither spontaneous nor casual but involved deliberate planning and composition (Rosenblum, 1989). Against this backdrop, the absence of a Boiler Annex from specific photographs is an unexplained inconsistency. The other buildings and structures are present in these photos, leaving us only to confirm that the Boiler Annex is indeed missing.

While it is clear that the Boiler Annex would have been integral to the event's infrastructure (Brown, 1999; Rydell, 1993), the reasons for its absence in some photographic records remain unknown. Another oddity is that our research could find no image of the two smokestacks producing smoke. A steam condenser discharge is commonly seen nearby but not from the smokestacks.

Were these hastily built late in the show to justify the massive electricity on display? Was the annex built but then not needed to produce electricity? Do they serve some other purpose that is secret or hidden from history?

MOBILE CAPACITORS OR BATTERIES

Secondly, an element that commands attention is the presence of unexplained electrical devices around the Court of Honor, as captured in some archival photographs. These objects, appearing as round structures closely resembling capacitors or batteries, show evidence of wiring. Their arrangement near lamp posts further emphasizes their apparent utility. These devices appear like direct current (DC) power boosters or supplemental power units, although the technology does not align with any well-documented systems of the time (Hughes, 1983; Nye, 1990).

The Court of Honor, as a focal point of the fair, would have required substantial electrical power for various functions, such as lighting and perhaps even special exhibits. One could surmise that the round devices might be related to these needs, but their absence in other historical records creates an enigma (Krajewski, 2014; Bijker, 1995).

Their existence provokes many questions, foremost among them: What experiments or demonstrations were these devices part of? Were they a form of early electrical storage or perhaps part of a power-boosting system that remained secret? Given that they do not resemble any standard-era technology (Marvin, 1988), could they have been part of a technological exhibition or an experiment in electrical engineering?

Or are they, perhaps, evidence of some other form of technology we are unfamiliar with?

Arthur Page Brown, Architect

Another subject inviting scrutiny is the role of Arthur Page Brown, an architect renowned for his contributions to the landscape of San Francisco. Brown is fascinating because, at the time of the 1894 California Midwinter International Exposition, he was also reportedly engaged in designing the San Francisco Ferry Building, a project of immense scale and importance. We are told that he designed both the California Building and the Mechanical Arts Building for the fair (Hitchcock, 1977; Starr, 2002).

The Ferry Building, aimed to be completed by 1896, was not just any project but was one of San Francisco's most significant architectural endeavors (Starr, 2007). It was intended to serve as a gateway to the city and would be characterized by its grandeur and functional utility, demanding substantial focus and commitment. Given the Ferry Building's scale and the attention it would have required, Brown's purported involvement in two high-profile, labor-intensive projects simultaneously is puzzling (King, 2009).

Architectural practice during this period was a detailed and laborious process involving the initial drawings and constant supervision, modification, and correspondence with other professionals like engineers and contractors (Saint, 1983). The designs for such grand projects would require many drafts, scale models, and an extensive understanding of materials and engineering principles (Wilson, 1996).

Not to belabor the point, but often in these narratives, we find the focus is on the architect; however, their involvement is often described fleetingly. It warrants a closer examination of what an architect in 1894 did, which will improve our understanding of this anomaly.

The number of architectural drawings required to detail a building so it can be constructed varies based on the complexity of the structure, its size, the number of different types of materials used, and other specialized requirements. For a building such as the many designed by A. Page Brown in the 1890s, one could expect a comprehensive set of drawings due to their intricate features. The Ferry building had several such as the arched arcade base, the state seal made of marble and mosaics, the 660-foot-long Great Nave, and the clock tower; and for the mechanical building its complex rounded dome and 300 feet width by 130 feet depth and grandiose outward façades.

In the architectural context of the 1896 Ferry Building and the 1894 Mechanical Arts Building, both designed by Arthur Page Brown, each deliverable's complexity and time requirements would be substantial. Here, we will break down the time needed for each type of architectural drawing and plan and along with the additional time required for revisions and coordination with engineers and builders.

Creating site plans for both structures would necessitate significant time investment. Brown would likely require approximately two weeks per project to complete this initial stage.

Site Plans = 4 weeks

Drafting the floor plans for both buildings would be an intricate task. Accounting for their differing layouts and functional requirements, it would take an estimated eight weeks to finalize these plans.

Floor Plans = 8 weeks

Producing the elevations for both buildings, including various views detailing the exterior features, would require an additional ten weeks.

Elevations = 10 weeks

Given these buildings' large-scale and multi-storied nature, about six weeks would be needed to produce detailed sectional views for both structures.

Sections = 6 weeks

Both buildings would feature high-quality materials and intricate architectural details. As a result, Brown would need approximately ten weeks to create these detailed drawings.

Detail Drawings = 10 weeks

Drafting the schedules, which list elements like windows and doors while specifying their types and sizes, would take roughly four weeks for both buildings.

Schedules = 4 weeks

Given these projects' advanced and cutting-edge implementations of electrical and plumbing systems, Brown would need around twelve weeks to develop these plans.

Electrical and Plumbing Plans = 12 weeks

The review and revision phase would also be significant, requiring approximately eight weeks to ensure the highest architectural drawings and plans quality.

Review and Revision = 8 weeks

Coordinating with engineers and builders during the construction phase of both projects would be complex and time-consuming. Brown would likely allocate about sixteen weeks for these coordination efforts.

Coordination with Engineers and Builders = 16 weeks

Adding up these labor summaries, the total time Brown would require for both projects would be 78 weeks.

Total Labor Summary: 78 weeks

Thus, under these assumptions, Arthur Page Brown would require 78 weeks to manage and execute both architectural projects comprehensively. Please realize that the above estimates are very conservative given the intricate nature of the buildings; it would not be surprising if the number of drawings ran into the hundreds.

Each building feature—specialized architectural elements, custom-designed components, or unique material applications—could require additional drawings to ensure accurate construction. A complex building with a great deal of custom work could easily require a substantial set of drawings, especially considering that all of these would have been produced by hand, increasing the need for clarity and detail (Ching, 2008).

However, two buildings at a time were nothing for Mr. Page; he was busy between 1888 and 1896 (when we are told he mysteriously died).

He completed the below list of projects in a short period (Arthur et al. (Architect), n.d.):

1. Mountain View Cemetery, Crocker, Charles, Monument, Oakland, CA - 1888
2. Crocker Old People's Home, Pacific Heights, San Francisco, CA - 1889-1890

3. Hibernia Savings and Loan Society, Office Building Project, Tenderloin, San Francisco, CA - 1890-1891
4. Episcopal Diocese of California, Trinity Church #4, San Francisco, CA - 1892-1893
5. World's Columbian Exposition, California Pavilion, Chicago, IL - 1892-1893
6. Atkinson Building, San Francisco, CA - 1892
7. Sainte Claire Club, Downtown, San Jose, CA - 1893-1894
8. California Mid-Winter Fair, Manufactures/Liberal Arts Building, San Francisco, CA - 1893-1894
9. Church of the New Jerusalem, Pacific Heights, San Francisco, CA - 1895
10. San Francisco Ferry Building, San Francisco, CA - 1896

For each project, an average of:

- Architectural Design: 30 weeks
- Coordination with Engineers: 8 weeks
- Material Calculation: 4 weeks
- Revisions: 6 weeks

Total per project = 30 (Design) + 8 (Engineering) + 4 (Materials) + 6 (Revisions) = 48 weeks

Labor Effort Equation for Refined Estimate: 10 projects x 48 weeks/project = 480 weeks

It is important to note that this estimate still simplifies the labor involved, as it does not account for contingencies, complexities specific to each project, or the architect's potential need to revisit projects for adjustments or troubleshooting during the construction phase. Therefore, the estimated 480 weeks should be considered a lower boundary rather than an exact duration.

Nevertheless, even with that said, 480 weeks is a little over nine years of continuous work with no breaks, no holidays, no illnesses, and no problems. So, Mr. Brown used up his luck as everything went perfectly for the first eight years of his profession until he was run over by a horse and buggy and was killed (Arthur et al. (Architect), n.d.). He must have had is head down in the thousands of architectural drawings he was producing at a breakneck pace as he ran from project to project, to busy to look both ways as he crossed the street.

WAS THE MIDWINTER FAIR ALREADY ESTABLISHED?

THE EXAMINER, SAN FRANCISCO: TUESDAY MORNING, JANUARY 10, 1893.

OPENING OF THE GREAT MID-WINTER SHOW.

President Stump Will Deliver the Inaugural Address at the Baldwin Theatre This Afternoon, and To-Night the Pavilion Will Shine in a Blaze of Glory.

10-DAY TELLS THE TALE.

Regents of the University to Meet This Afternoon.

WILL PROF. MOSES BE EL'CTED?

Members of the Board Speak for Moses

Newspaper.com Archive

The presence of an article in the San Francisco Examiner dated January 10, 1893, discussing the opening of a "great mid-winter show" provides concrete evidence that an event by that name existed prior to the Mid-Winter Fair of 1894. In the image above of the headline, note the date of January 10, 1893. Also note the reference that the pavilion will "Shine in a Blaze of Glory," denoting that electrical lighting was already present a year before the 1894 fair on the show grounds.

This brings into focus the glaring inconsistencies of the official narrative.

For example, official accounts suggest that the founder of the 1894 Mid-Winter Fair, Michael H. de Young, returned from the Chicago Fair in August of 1893 and had just 157 days to plan and execute the event. As we have proven, this time frame would be implausibly short for constructing an entire fairground from scratch. We believe we have proven that the 1894 fair was not conceived of and built from the ground up in 157 days.

However, consider this: If the Mid-Winter event were an annual happening, many of these inconsistencies and timelines would make more sense. Existing infrastructure would already be in place, requiring some updates or modifications for the 1894 event. This would make the 157-day time frame from conception to execution for the 1894 fair much more plausible. The idea that the Mid-Winter Fair was an annual event solves many logistical inconsistencies in the timeline.

The above headline proves that it was.

Nevertheless, this leads to an even more perplexing question: Why would the official narrative deliberately obscure or falsify this information? What purpose would it serve to claim the 1894 event as a brand new, standalone affair when evidence proves it was part of an ongoing series of events? Such a discrepancy between the narrative and evidence might imply an attempt to portray the 1894 fair as an exceptional, unprecedented event.

However, the question remains: Why go to the lengths of crafting an impossible story, like building the entire fair in 157 days, when they could readily admit that it was part of an ongoing tradition?

The possible reasons for this discrepancy could be multiple and complex, including political, social, or economic motivations that favored presenting the fair as a unique, singular event.

Could this start to disclose the elusive motive we have been searching for? It provides some concrete evidence that the narrative was changed, and we can start to see the pattern of reasoning. There was something about the location of this fair that the people who created the historical narrative wanted to be hidden.

Was it that they did not want to draw attention to the fact that this location already had buildings and infrastructure on it?

We need to start treating this analysis as a formal investigation. It might be time to bring in tried and true modern forensic methodologies.

CHAPTER 9: EVIDENCE OF THE OLD WORLD
ONE YEAR WONDERS

CATALOGING THE IMPOSSIBLE NARRATIVES

In the preceding chapter, we presented compelling evidence questioning the widely accepted timeline and narrative of the 1894 Midwinter Fair in San Francisco. More than compelling, we feel it completely dismantles the narrative. We believe our in-depth analysis successfully raises enough questions that it is reasonable to assume, at least concerning San Francisco up through 1894, that the sequence of actual events in its founding and build-out are, at their most generous, not in the chronological order we are currently given.

We also note that we can no longer be constrained by this false timeline in our syntopical analysis. We cannot allow ourselves to fall into the Distraction Ploy, where we work at a micro level, moving anomalies around under the umbrella of the broader falsehood we have uncovered. Such discrepancies can no longer be dismissed as mere anomalies; there are too many, and the events, once critically examined, are too impossible to accept.

To move forward, we will adopt several more assumptions to our investigation. First, we will start looking for broader patterns in the narratives; second, we will allow our criticisms to expand to an intersection of these broader patterns and physical objects mentioned within the narrative (like buildings); and third, we will bring in a tried-and-true investigative framework as we work to uncover how and why the actual history and established narrative may not align.

We will integrate the framework of means, motive, and opportunity, commonly used in the field of criminal justice (Turvey, 2011), into the specific context of our historical inquiry.

MEANS: THE RESOURCES REQUIRED FOR ALTERING THE NARRATIVE

The first area to be aware of is "means," encompassing the array of resources and capabilities needed to shape or direct an official historical narrative concerning the early history of San Francisco. The question of means extends beyond altering or forging documents, including creating new, officially sanctioned documents that embed a false narrative. In such a scenario, the persons or organizations involved would not necessarily need to engage in forgery; instead, they could use their positions of authority or expertise to produce seemingly legitimate historical records.

To better understand this, we must consider the context of the time. Would these individuals have had access to the means of producing textual or visual documents? Would they have been in positions where they could influence or control the archival process, thereby facilitating the acceptance of these documents as part of the historical record? Additionally, were they in a financial position to undertake such activities, given that publishing and disseminating records would require monetary resources?

These questions necessitate an examination of multiple elements: the prevailing technology, the social and professional networks that could be leveraged to disseminate these records, and the economic circumstances of the parties involved (Tosh, 2008).

By examining "means" in this multifaceted manner, we aim to ascertain whether the individuals or groups implicated had the necessary resources to introduce a new or modified narrative into the official historical account of the early history of San Francisco. This foundational understanding will allow us to tackle the subsequent components of motive and opportunity.

MOTIVE: THE UNDERLYING REASONS FOR CHANGING THE STORY

As we inspect the concept of "motive" for shaping or directing the early history of San Francisco, we must acknowledge the inherent challenges of definitively ascertaining these underlying incentives. Despite our best efforts to explore the potential political, economic, ideological, and personal motives, it is crucial to recognize that motive might ultimately remain elusive and, in some cases, impenetrable (Elton, 2002).

Political, economic, or ideological interests can be inferred through primary and secondary source materials, such as government documents, personal correspondences, and media publications from the relevant time period. However, these sources offer, at best, a lens through which we might glimpse the motivations of those involved. They do not provide conclusive proof, especially when considering that the individuals or organizations responsible could have had multifaceted, overlapping motives that a single document could not capture (Tosh, 2008).

Moreover, the absence of a clear motive does not necessarily negate the act of shaping history itself. The early history of San Francisco could have been altered or directed for reasons that have been lost to time, intentionally obscured, or are so complex that they defy straightforward analysis. Sometimes, the motives may be so deeply ingrained within the cultural or social fabric of the time that they escape contemporary interpretation (Windschuttle, 2009).

Even personal motives, seemingly the most straightforward to understand, can be clouded by the subjectivity of human behavior and emotion and the distance of time. Ambitions like career advancement or academic recognition could coexist with more altruistic desires, making pinpointing a single, overriding motive challenging.

So, while our investigation aims to explore the multiple angles from which one might be motivated to shape the early history of San Francisco, we must proceed with the understanding that the full scope of such motives may only partially be known or understood. This nuanced stance does not diminish the importance of our inquiry into motive; instead, it adds a layer of complexity that makes our subsequent exploration of means and opportunity even more critical for understanding how the narrative of San Francisco's early history might have been influenced.

If we can show the means existed, and the opportunity existed, and significant narratives like the history given for the 1894 Midwinter Exhibition are proven false, meaning the history has been altered, we can explore motives with a better understanding of what we are looking for.

OPPORTUNITY: THE FEASIBILITY OF ALTERING HISTORICAL WORKS

As we continue our exploration through the framework of means, motive, and now "opportunity," we pivot our attention towards a different angle. Specifically, we examine patterns in the historical narrative alongside the physical structures in San Francisco to evaluate the likelihood that the city's early history was shaped or directed (Turvey, 2011).

We have already proven that the patterns in the narrative deserve scrutiny. Narratives that repeatedly emphasize or omit specific details, events, or characters could indicate an intentional effort to shape historical understanding. For example, if multiple accounts depict a particular period or event in San Francisco's history similarly, this pattern could point to a directed narrative despite evidence to the contrary. Such consistency across different sources might not be a mere coincidence but rather an indicator of an opportunity to alter or shape the accepted historical record (Tosh, 2008).

Turning to physical structures, like buildings, can serve as tangible touchstones against which to compare and evaluate the historical narrative. Preserved, altered, or even demolished buildings can carry historical significance that either aligns with or contradicts the accepted story. If, for example, a preserved building's established history does not align with its architectural style or materials, that incongruence could indicate an opportunity where the shaping of the narrative may have occurred (Elton, 2002).

Moreover, institutions that maintain these physical structures, such as historical societies or preservation committees, could play a pivotal role. If these organizations possess either the means or motive, their stewardship over these buildings could have allowed them to adjust or create records, plaques, or even guided tours that propagate a particular narrative (Windschuttle, 2009).

While it's challenging to establish motive definitively, the convergence of narrative patterns and the state of physical buildings in San Francisco makes the shaping of its early history not just plausible but likely. This nuanced examination of opportunity, in tandem with previously discussed means and the elusive nature of motive, solidifies our overall framework (Turvey, 2011) and suggests a high likelihood that the city's early history was deliberately shaped, which we will prove in the following sections of this chapter.

Our careful analysis has uncovered a pattern that prompts further inquiry into San Francisco's early architectural history. The juxtaposition of means, motive, and opportunity is a robust analytical framework that will allow us to organize data, lending credence to the likelihood that San Francisco's historical narrative has been deliberately crafted. This prepares us for the subsequent, more specialized layer of our research.

To get started, one consistent pattern stands out: many of San Francisco's iconic buildings are said to have been rapidly built, swiftly destroyed, and then quickly rebuilt—sometimes going through two or three such cycles—all before 1906. Given the technological limitations of the era and the scale of these buildings, such a timeline is highly improbable.

This notable inconsistency in the historical accounts provides fertile ground for our upcoming investigation. We will scrutinize these rapidly constructed, deconstructed, and reconstructed buildings using the analytical triad of means, motive, and opportunity. Each building we present involves an impossible narrative: its construction timetable. Using the 1894 Midwinter Exposition as our analytical template, each of these buildings' narratives could be deconstructed similarly. At the same time, we may return to these structures and do just that in some future research; we believe here that simply presenting the construction narrative makes our point ten-fold.

BUILDINGS WITH DODGY NARRATIVES

THE BALDWIN HOTEL

The Baldwin Hotel

The conventional understanding is that the Baldwin Hotel was constructed in 1875 within one year (Dillon, 1983). The building, encompassing an area of approximately 200,000 square feet, was designed to serve as a luxury hotel. Built primarily using bricks and ornate wooden embellishments for its interior, the Baldwin Hotel exhibited an intricate blend of Victorian architectural elements (Lotchin, 2003).

The Baldwin Theatre

The Baldwin Hotel was destroyed in the great fire of 1906 on April 18, 1906, after standing for 31 years (Lotchin, 2003).

The Baldwin from Market Street

FLOOD BUILDING

Flood Building

The Flood Building in San Francisco began construction in 1903 and was completed in 1904; it was designed by architect Albert Pissis (Lotchin, 2002). It is one of the few structures that survived the catastrophic 1906 San Francisco Earthquake and subsequent fires, demonstrating its resilience and robust construction. The building was built in a Beaux-Arts architectural style and featured steel frame construction with exterior walls made of Colusa sandstone (King, 2004). It covers an area of approximately 350,000 square feet.

Flood Building Interior, Modern

Flood Building, Modern

CENTRAL TOWER

Newspaper Row, Central Tower on Right

The Central Tower, initially known as the Call Building, was constructed in San Francisco in 1898 within a timeframe of approximately one year (Corbett, 1979). Spanning 15 floors and covering roughly 300,000 square feet, the building was an architectural marvel of its time, designed in the Renaissance Revival style. Predominantly constructed of steel frames with a terracotta façade, the building's intricate details and large scale stand out compared to other early skyscrapers (Lewis, 2007).

Central Tower from Market Street

The building was designed as a commercial edifice, housing the San Francisco Call newspaper, among other businesses and offices. Over time, it transformed into a multi-tenant office space, serving various industries and contributing to the business ecosystem of San Francisco (Moses, 2002).

Contrary to many of its contemporaries who succumbed to the various disasters that befell San Francisco, the Central Tower survived but underwent significant renovations. The most noteworthy renovation occurred in 1938, when the building was modernized, and its external ornamentation was largely removed (San et al. Department, 2014).

THE PALACE HOTEL

The Palace Hotel, 1875

The Palace Hotel in San Francisco was constructed in 1875 within a span of approximately one year (Lotchin, 2003). The grand and elegant hotel comprised seven stories and contained around 800 rooms. It covered an estimated 600,000 square feet of floor space.

The Bar of the original Palace Hotel

The hotel featured a blend of Victorian and French Second Empire design elements (Dillon, 1983). The building's principal construction materials were brick, marble, and wood, complemented by intricate plaster moldings and expansive glass installations, further adding layers of complexity to the design.

Palace Hotel Courtyard

Grand Victoria and Palace Hotel (Right)

The original structure was destroyed on April 18, 1906, and existed for approximately 31 years. We are told the building was rebuilt in the exact same spot after the fire using the same materials.

SAN FRANCISCO PUBLIC LIBRARY

The San Francisco Public Library's original building was constructed in 1890 within an estimated timeframe of one year (Roberts, 1995). Spanning ten floors with an approximate floor space of 100,000 square feet, the library was a notable structure made predominantly of brick and sandstone, in a style reminiscent of Classical Revival architecture (Williams, 2007).

The San Francisco Public Library was designed to be a repository for books, manuscripts, and various other forms of information. It served as an educational hub, providing free access to knowledge for the citizens of San Francisco. Throughout its existence, the library held significant cultural and educational value, contributing to the city's intellectual growth and functioning as a public space for learning (Lotchin, 2003).

The original structure of the San Francisco Public Library was destroyed on April 18, 1906, having existed for approximately 16 years. We are told the library was rebuilt on the exact same spot with the same materials.

HIBERNIA BANK BUILDING

Hibernia Bank Building, Modern

The Hibernia Bank Building in San Francisco was constructed in 1892, and the construction process was reportedly completed within a single year (Johnson, 1996). With its Beaux-Arts architectural style, the structure was grand and elegant, featuring a dome, large windows, and intricate stone carvings. Spanning approximately 40,000 square feet, the building was primarily made of sandstone and marble (Smith, 2002).

Hibernia Bank Building, Interior

The building was initially used as a banking facility and played a critical role in San Francisco's financial sector during the late 19th and early 20th centuries (Kern, 2004). As a bank, it served not only individual customers but also various businesses that were vital to the local economy.

JAMES C. FLOOD MANSION

James C. Flood Mansion, Modern

The James C. Flood Mansion, located in San Francisco, was built in 1886, and the construction was reportedly completed within the same year (O'Brien, 1992). The building is a classic example of the Italianate style and features intricate ornamentation, high ceilings, and grand staircases. Covering an area of about 30,000 square feet, the building was primarily constructed of brownstone, marble, and various hardwoods (Clark, 1998).

James C. Flood Mansion Steps, Modern

The mansion was primarily used as a residence for James C. Flood, a notable business magnate of the era, and his family. The edifice symbolized social prestige and economic might during the late 19th-century San Francisco. As such, it stood as an architectural marvel and a signifier of the economic vitality of the Flood family and, by extension, the burgeoning capitalist society of the city (Richardson, 2003).

1850, ST. FRANCIS HOTEL

St. Francis Hotel, Modern

The St. Francis Hotel was constructed in 1850 in less than a year (Hart, 1991). The building operated for less than a year when it was destroyed in a fire in 1850 (Smith, 2005). It was rebuilt in one year in 1904, right before the 1906 earthquake, and rebuilt after the earthquake (Lotchin, 1997), we are told, using the exact same materials.

1850, JENNY LIND THEATRE

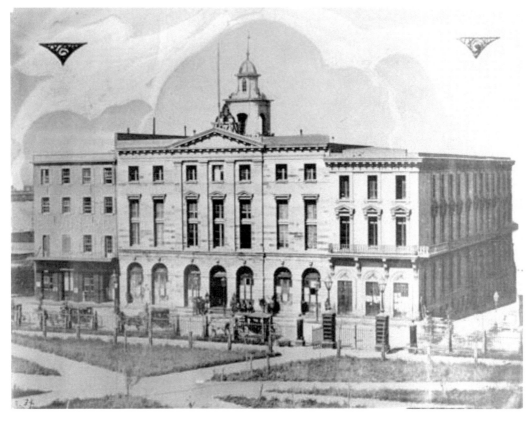

1850, Jenny Lind Theatre

The Jenny Lind Theatre was constructed in 1850 in one year (Hart, 1991), driven by the relentless belief that a high-end theater was what the emerging gold rush town needed. It then burned down and was rebuilt in 1851 in one year, which burned down that same year, and a third building (pictured) was built in one year and went into operation in 1851 (Smith, 2005). Yes, the narrative is that it was built three times in a year each over the course of two years. Then, after failing immediately as a theater in 1852, it became the San Francisco City Hall until the early 1870s, when it fell into disrepair (Isenberg, 2005).

1851, SAN FRANCISCO CUSTOMS HOUSE

1851, San Francisco Customs House

The San Francisco Customs House was constructed in 1851, with the building process spanning one year (Thompson, 1999). It was strategically located near the city's harbor, an essential factor considering its function as a federal establishment in charge of monitoring and regulating maritime trade (Nelson, 2002).

It served as a governmental facility designed to oversee the collection of customs duties, enforce trade laws, and provide documentation for imports and exports. It was essential in regulating maritime commerce, crucial for the federal government's revenue and the local economy (Johnson, 2003). Its role was economic and symbolic, representing federal oversight and authority at a pivotal time in San Francisco's development as a major port city (Smith, 2004).

The San Francisco Customs House was destroyed in 1866 after standing for only 15 years (Davis, 2005).

1854, OLD SAINT MARY'S CATHEDRAL

Old Saint Mary's Cathedral, Modern

Old St. Mary's Cathedral was constructed in the heart of San Francisco's Chinatown, with construction commencing in 1853 and completed in one year in 1854 (Osborne, 2005). A significant aspect of the building's construction was the use of granite blocks brought from China as a primary building material, which was both durable and aesthetically pleasing (Chiu, 1997).

Old Saint Mary's Cathedral, Interior

The church was consecrated in 1854 by Archbishop Joseph Alemany, and its completion was a milestone for the Roman Catholic community in San Francisco, which had, until that point, been without a cathedral (Corbett, 2003).

Old U.S. Mint (Mint Plaza)

Old U.S. Mint (Mint Plaza), 1874

The Old U.S. Mint in San Francisco, also known as the "Granite Lady," was constructed over a period of approximately one year between 1854 and 1855. Architect Alfred B. Mullett designed the building in a Greek Revival style, featuring a robust granite facade that lent the building its nickname (Brechin, 1999).

The Old U.S. Mint has undergone various well-known renovations. One of the most significant renovations occurred in 1973 when the building was converted into the San Francisco Museum at the Mint. The renovation aimed to preserve the historical integrity of the building while modernizing its facilities for public engagement (Myrick, 1992). Another vital renovation in 2003 focused on structural updates and restorations to ensure the building met current safety standards (Lee, 2004).

GRACE CATHEDRAL

Grace Cathedral, Modern Day, Front

The Grace Cathedral in San Francisco was initially constructed in 1849, with the first structure completed within a year (Willis, 2008). The structure is mainly built from reinforced concrete, which is then clad in limestone, covering an area of approximately 93,400 square feet (Davis, 1999).

Grace Cathedral, Modern Day, Back

MECHANICS' INSTITUTE BUILDING

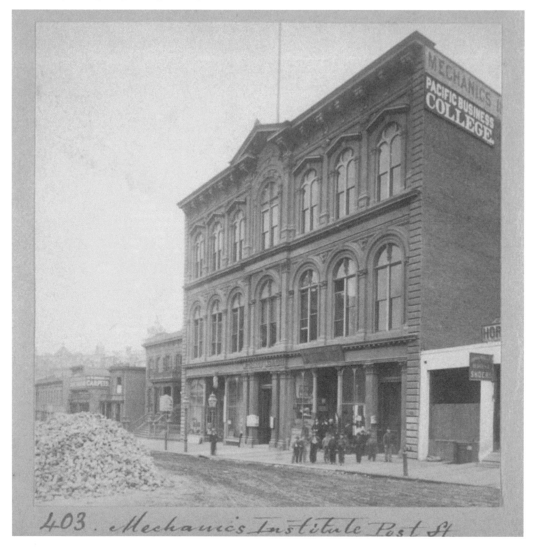

Mechanics' Institute Building

The Mechanics' Institute Building was constructed in 1854 in San Francisco over the course of one year. The building housed a library, lecture halls, and other educational facilities, serving as a hub for disseminating technical knowledge, skills training, and community engagement (Case, 2010). The Mechanics' Institute Building was destroyed on May 3, 1906.

THE PARROTT BUILDING

The Parrott Building

The Parrott Building was constructed in 1852 and constructed within that year in San Francisco (Hart, 1991). The Parrott Building was destroyed on May 3, 1853. It lasted approximately one year before its destruction (Isenberg, 2005).

CALVARY PRESBYTERIAN CHURCH

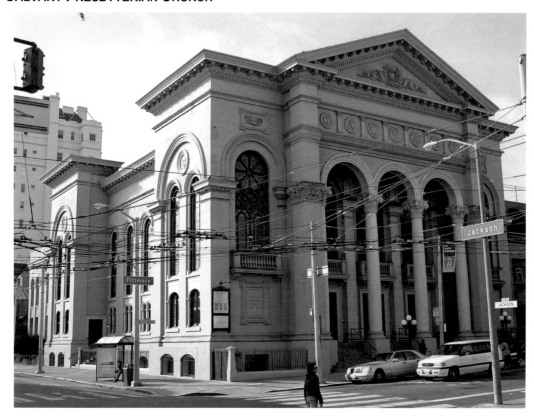

Calvary Presbyterian Church

The Old First Presbyterian Church was established in San Francisco in 1854 and took approximately one year to complete its construction (Brechin, 2006). It occupied a space of approximately 22,000 square feet (Meyer, 1990). The original building was destroyed in the earthquake and subsequent fires of 1906 after standing for 52 years (Thompson, 2001; Johnson, 2006). We are told it was rebuilt using the same materials.

THE MARK HOPKINS MANSION

The Mark Hopkins Mansion

The Mark Hopkins Mansion in San Francisco was erected in 1878, with the construction reportedly completed within that same year (Miller, 1995). This impressive building showcased the opulence of the late 19th-century architectural style, characterized by grand rooms, intricate woodwork, and ornate chandeliers. The mansion spanned a generous 40,000 square feet and was predominantly built with redwood, granite, and brick (Gray, 2004).

The mansion was primarily designed as a residence for Mark Hopkins, one of the "Big Four" who were instrumental in building the Central Pacific Railroad. As such, it served as a domicile and a symbol of Hopkins' immense wealth and social standing (Phillips, 2007).

The Mark Hopkins Mansion was destroyed on April 18, 1906. The building stood for approximately 28 years before meeting its end (Johnson, 2010).

The Mark Hopkins Mansion, Interior

TEMPLE EMANU-EL ON SUTTER STREET

Temple Emanu-El on Sutter Street

Temple Emanu-El on Sutter Street in San Francisco was constructed in 1864 and was completed within that same year (Goldman, 1989). The building was primarily constructed using bricks and limestone (Schneider, 2001). Its internal structure featured wooden trusses to support the roof. The synagogue covered an approximate area of 12,000 square feet, an expansive size given the technological and logistical constraints of the 1860s (Jackson, 1995).

The architectural style was Moorish Revival, characterized by horseshoe arches, intricate moldings, and geometric patterns. It was a structure that stood out for its spiritual significance and aesthetic grandiosity, featuring a significant dome and two lofty towers on either side of the main entrance (Schneider, 2001).

Temple Emanu-El on Sutter Street, Interior

Temple Emanu-El served as a house of worship, an educational center, and a social gathering place for the Jewish community in San Francisco (Levenson, 1997). Its function extended beyond the religious domain to include a robust role in the cultural and community life of San Francisco's Jewish population.

The building was destroyed on April 18, 1906, and had stood for approximately 42 years before its destruction (Williams, 2010).

CHAPTER 10: THE NARRATIVE

WWPMD

WHAT WOULD PERRY MASON DO?

"That is not skillful lying. It is not the proper way to commit perjury. The skillful perjurer is he who sticks to so much of the truth as is possible, and only departs from it when it becomes absolutely necessary. These men who make up stories out of whole cloth usually leave a few loose threads somewhere. Yet it is a strange thing about the human mind: It has many facts constantly thrust upon it, and it doesn't properly correlate those facts. I had the facts at my command for some time before I knew what must have happened"

- *Perry Mason (Gardner, 1934).*

The wise words of fictional trial lawyer Perry Mason remind us of the complex interplay between truth and deceit. Like a skilled impostor, history, it seems, weaves a story that mixes facts with hidden truths. Mason's insightful observation about the human mind's ability to connect facts correctly resonates with the anomalies of the 1800s that we have examined in this book. In this final chapter, we will revisit the evidence and anomalies presented, not as separate threads but as woven fabric, asking you, the reader, to consider what "really happened."

Just like Mason, we have systematically gathered and presented evidence for analysis. Now, it is time to connect the dots, tie the loose ends, and challenge the official narratives passed on to us. While some anomalies may remain unexplainable, their existence compels us to scrutinize them even more rigorously to get as close to the truth as possible.

What would Perry Mason do if faced with such a complex historical puzzle?

He would likely begin by scrutinizing the anomalies and inconsistencies, however minor they might appear.

He would then dissect these discrepancies, not to negate the broader narrative, but to refine and enrich his understanding of the true events that transpired.

By holding up each piece of evidence up to the light and questioning its place in the story, Mason would aim to resolve ambiguities and bring a more nuanced picture of events to the fore.

As we move through this concluding chapter, let us adopt a similar approach. Let us evaluate our evidence rigorously, question conventional narratives, and seek to build a more coherent and evidence-based understanding of the history in question.

In a Perry Mason case, we often find resolution in a dramatic courtroom confession or an irrefutable piece of evidence that ties all loose ends. In our historical investigation, however, we must accept that we may not arrive at such neat conclusions. The "witnesses" in our case are long gone, and the "evidence" has often been mediated through time, multiple interpretations, and sometimes even deliberate obfuscation. While we may not have a courtroom to compel a confession or conclusively prove a theory, we do have the power of rigorous academic inquiry.

Through this lens, we will continue to probe, question, and analyze, always seeking a clearer picture of the past, even if that image remains somewhat elusive. Thus, we move forward, not in search of a dramatic finale but of a deeper, more nuanced understanding of the historical questions and complexities we have examined.

HISTORY MIGHT NOT BE WHAT WE THINK IT IS

We began by discussing the expedition of Juan Rodríguez Cabrillo, a Portuguese explorer sailing for the Spanish Crown. It was noted that San Francisco was believed to have been named by Spanish explorers in honor of St. Francis of Assisi in the late 18th century.

However, an inconsistency in this narrative was pointed out.

When consulting 16th and 17th-century maps from France, it was discovered that San Francisco was named and located in California almost a century before the Spanish explorers' supposed discovery. As there was no known link between the name 'S. Francisco' on these maps and any pre-Columbian Native American cultures, it was concluded that the name must have been adopted from whoever was present near modern-day San Francisco when new people moved into the region.

This led to a more profound mystery when Urbano Monte's 1587 map was examined.

The 1587 map depicted many cities and towns across the North American continent; some appeared to be temporary settlements, while others were shown as cities surrounded by walls and barriers with almost skyscraper-looking buildings. This contrast raised questions about the true nature of these cities and the infrastructure level in America at the time.

Our exploration continued with the mysterious disappearance of the Roanoke Colony in the late 16th century. A map created by the colony's governor, John White, provided important geographical information but concealed a significant detail. Beneath a patch on the map, modern scanning techniques revealed a drawing of a star fort, a strategic military structure associated with the Renaissance period.

However, again, this new discovery led to more mysteries.

Where did the shared knowledge or technology to build such forts come from? Why were these structures consistently failing in their primary function as defensive establishments despite the considerable resources invested in their construction?

It was concluded that a substantial reevaluation of North American history might be necessary. Whether it is reshaping the story of San Francisco's naming or investigating the cities and forts seen in old maps, or digging deeply into maps' like John Whites to discover new information, numerous areas required in-depth exploration and study.

We investigated the fascinating mysteries surrounding Meriwether Lewis and William Clark's expedition, its objectives, and its connection to San Francisco.

President Thomas Jefferson commissioned Lewis and Clark in the early 1800s to explore the newly acquired Louisiana Purchase and find a route to the Pacific Ocean. Despite their intensive documentation efforts, their maps faced criticism for their primitive nature compared to contemporaneous sketches.

Why weren't skilled map makers sent on this important assignment?

We questioned why their cartography was of lower quality than John White's charting of Roanoke in 1590, despite being two centuries earlier. The Lewis and Clark expedition occurred after the Louisiana Purchase, a strategic move by influential American political and business figures to secure trade pathways and heighten security and expansion opportunities. This led us to speculate if prior knowledge or subtle cues about the area's potential had been available to them.

We then returned to San Francisco proper, marked on their map as 'S. Francisco,' despite not being directly explored by Lewis and Clark. We noted how it aligns with our contemporary understanding of its geographical location. Another notable feature on their chart points west to the 'Port of Sir Frances Drake,' identifying another layer of historical involvement with the region.

We discussed Sir Francis Drake's role in English exploration, including his circumnavigation feats and his influence on defeating the Spanish Armada. His landing on the California coast in 1579 became the center of our discussion, as it is believed to be Drake's Cove in Marin County or as southward as the San Francisco Bay, despite unclear historical documentation.

We found it intriguing that Lewis and Clark marked the Port of Sir Frances Drake on their map, referencing the bay where San Francisco is located today, despite subsequent explorers reportedly missing it for centuries. We questioned the conventional understanding of the reasons behind this dilemma, exploring whether narrow bay entrances, foggy weather conditions, and coastal currents are adequate explanations given the seasoned mariners' navigational skills and familiarity with tricky waters.

Our investigation showed strong evidence that Sir Francis Drake discovered and named San Francisco Bay, consistent with his exploration practices—the appearance of 'S. Francisco' and 'Port of Sir Frances Drake' on the 1669 Map Amerique Septentrionale and Lewis and Clark's map support our hypothesis. This presents an inquiry into the motives behind the altered historical narrative and the beneficiaries it serves today.

While expanding our investigation to Fort Point in San Francisco, we encountered some peculiarities and contradictions that challenged the accepted historical narrative of not just this structure but San Francisco as a whole. We used the method of syntopical analysis to trace the fort's history, and we found several perplexing issues.

Firstly, we discovered that the fort's intricate and complex masonry was of the Third System design, typically used for forts on the East Coast that were under a different threat environment. It was odd that Fort Point was the only such structure on the West Coast that adhered to this design, especially for a city swarming with gold prospectors during the gold rush.

We also found puzzling inconsistencies in the fort's construction history.

According to historical narratives, the granite used for Fort Point's foundation was imported from China. However, it seemed highly improbable that this was the case, given the availability of local alternatives. We calculated that it would have required an unreasonable number of ships to transport the necessary amount of granite from China, especially considering the complexities and costs of international trade in the 19th century.

Furthermore, the narrative told us that gold prospectors suddenly became master masons, which seems questionable given the profound differences between the two crafts. The construction timeline also highlights the improbability of the project's completion within the stipulated eight years. All these factors contribute to the improbability of the narrative.

The Third System design strategy used at Fort Point failed in several instances during the Civil War on the East Coast. It appears to have been too expensive, overly complex, and ultimately ineffective for the threats it faced. Therefore, it seems bizarre that the design was implemented at Fort Point, given its strategic position on the West Coast.

Our inquiry revealed several inconsistencies and raised numerous questions about the Fort Point narrative, so we researched the construction of Fort Point in San Francisco during the 1850s. Despite the limitations of that time, the military made remarkably advanced choices, which led us to explore the historical context further. We also investigated the acquisition of Alcatraz Island by the U.S. government in 1846, a strategic move that only became apparent after the California Gold Rush of 1848. The sequence of events seemed unusual and hinted at a Distraction Ploy, masking the larger narrative.

Once a peaceful settlement, San Francisco underwent significant growth during this time because of the Gold Rush. The influx of people led to increased demand for infrastructure. We conducted a thorough analysis of the city's resilience in rebuilding after a series of fires destroyed its urban landscape between 1849 and 1851. We were especially interested in the source of materials used for the reconstructions, particularly the shift from timber to fire-resistant bricks.

After reviewing the historical narrative, we noticed that the events seemed out of order and raised questions about the accurate chronology of San Francisco's history. Additionally, we identified a potential Distraction Ploy, which could divert attention away from the primary deception within a narrative. To effectively counter this ploy, we recommended a holistic, Syntopical approach that critically evaluates the foundational premise of all information.

Using this Syntopical methodology, we examined the perplexing choice to build Fort Point with highly advanced materials and technologies for its time. The common belief is that the city's six devastating fires greatly impacted its architectural development. Although this explains the overall shift from timber to brick structures, it also necessitated a massive reconstruction effort that would have competed with the militaries objectives.

During the rebuilding of San Francisco, numerous challenges related to the demand for bricks existed. The production process required vast resources and labor, making it a highly complex logistical task. Given the repeated disasters, including fires and earthquakes, it was hard to imagine how San Francisco procured enough bricks.

After the devastating fires, we delved into the significance of using bricks and related resources to construct buildings in San Francisco. We examined the process of brickmaking in the 1850s, highlighting the various roles involved. Although brick construction was promoted as a solution to fire damage, we discovered inconsistencies in the information about this material and the timeline.

Ultimately, the unpredictable development of San Francisco in the 1850s, driven by urgent reconstruction requirements and changing building materials, left us with several questions about the accuracy of the narrative and the intricate nature of these developments.

During our investigation, we analyzed four major primary sources: the 1849 William M. Eddy survey of San Francisco, the 1859 U.S. Coastal Survey map of San Francisco, and visual images of Fort Point from 1856 and the Merchant Exchange Building from 1851.

We examined the 1849 survey of San Francisco and were amazed by the precise and forward-thinking depiction of the city's future expansion. The grid system was meticulously designed. It included streets that had not been built and, in some cases, on land that was underwater at the time. This raised questions about the capabilities of a 19th-centruy surveyor and his apparent prophetic vision.

We discovered some intriguing inconsistencies when we analyzed the 1859 U.S. Coastal Survey map of San Francisco. The survey showed an 89-foot sand dune on Market Street, which had already been developed, challenging the historical timeline and highlighting the possible inconsistencies when relying solely on secondary sources for historical narratives.

Furthermore, we found photographs of Fort Point that revealed the structure was already completed in 1856, contradicting the accepted construction timeline—the absence of any signs of recent construction or maritime support added to the mystery surrounding this finding.

The Merchant Exchange Building's sophisticated design gave an impression of advancement that seemed inconsistent with the time in which it was built, posing further questions. We found anomalies that challenged established secondary narratives as we examined primary sources. This required re-evaluating long-standing historical interpretations, potentially requiring alignment with primary sources, and thoroughly reexamining the entire historical framework. Our analysis emphasized the importance of engaging directly with primary sources to connect with raw, unmediated information. This way, we could avoid the Distraction Ploy to reinforce the importance of understanding context and preserve academic integrity.

Examining primary sources exposed a fundamental issue in the accepted timeline of historical events related to San Francisco, hinting toward a potential revision of historical understanding. This highlighted the value of primary sources and their role in shaping our understanding of the past.

We then moved into a broader context, reviewing the Centennial Exposition of 1876, the first significant World's Fair in the United States, held in Philadelphia. We wanted to examine other large-scale building projects to see if they too had the same inconsistencies. The fair held symbolic importance for a nation grappling with post-Civil War reconstruction, and we also acknowledged the contribution of smaller exhibitions that set the stage for larger international events.

Our investigation covered a range of fairs, including the 1851 Great Exhibition in London, which served as a blueprint for future events of this kind. We considered both the positive and negative narratives surrounding these exhibitions, including critiques that argued they reinforced industrial and imperial authority. We also looked at the 1867 Exposition Universelles in Paris, celebrated for its showcase of groundbreaking inventions against the backdrop of a city known for culture and advancement.

We scrutinized logistical aspects, such as the rapid assembly and dismantling of monumental buildings and exhibits and explored potential alternative viewpoints beyond mainstream historical accounts. Our investigations extended to confirming attendance figures, inspecting provisions made for the surging crowds, and challenging the astonishing speed at which iconic edifices like the Crystal Palace were constructed.

Our survey of fairs concluded with a focus on the 1876 Centennial Exposition in Philadelphia, the 1893 World's Columbian Exposition in Chicago, and the 1894 California Midwinter International Exposition in San Francisco. While acknowledging the role of these events in elevating cultural and economic status, we raised concerns about the practicality of hosting events of such magnitude.

We discovered a recurring theme of awe and skepticism surrounding these grand exhibitions. While widely celebrated for their logistical, architectural, and financial achievements, we aimed to dig deeper, posing questions not commonly addressed in current academic discourse. Our intent was to offer a richer contextual understanding of these pivotal events without undermining their historical significance.

We extensively researched the history of the 1894 California Midwinter International Exposition, which is also known as the Midwinter Fair. The traditional account was based on well-known secondary sources that aimed to provide a thorough but conventional understanding of the event, with a focus on its economic aspects. The goal of this analysis was to establish a basic understanding of this significant exposition.

Our journey into 1894 started with the birth of the 1894 Midwinter Fair, designed to strengthen San Francisco's economic and cultural status. This magnificent event lasted 159 days, featuring more than 120 buildings carefully constructed on 200 acres of the now-famous Golden Gate Park. We were impressed that it showcased not only the progress and achievements of America but also welcomed the involvement of 38 international participants.

When considering the feasibility and impact of the event, we focused on its financial aspects. Our analysis revealed that the narrative of cost was a substantial amount, approximately $1,193,260.70, which was significant for that period. The main source of revenue was the sale of tickets, which generated a total revenue of $3,177,965.75. However, upon closer examination, we discovered that the staffing costs associated with the event were quite high. Disproportionately high. As a result, the revenue was considerably outweighed by the staffing expenses.

In addition, we deemed it important to consider the financial deficit in the larger economic landscape of California and the entire United States at that time. Our research indicated that such a substantial monetary loss would have had a major impact on the economy of California in the late 1800s, which would have made the efforts of the fair organizers even more futile, thus questioning the odd historical positivity around an event that in reality was a financial disaster of epic proportions.

We further explored the challenges of organizing a large exhibition and the logistics involved. In 1894, San Francisco had a population of only 298,000, yet the exhibition had to accommodate over 2.22 million visitors and employees. This presented a monumental task, especially considering the limited hospitality infrastructure available. Additionally, we are told there were huge numbers of workers, so much so that they exceeded the city's population more than twofold, raising concerns about how they were sourced and accommodated.

The Midwinter Fair, seemingly an exercise in irony, was an ambitious effort towards economic revival amidst the Panic of 1893 yet concurrently an illustration of economic overreaching at a time of severe financial crisis. Publisher Michael H. de Young organized the event with the help of other influential individuals to revive the local economy and showcase California's agricultural abundance.

The fair celebrated arts, culture, technology, and science, with the Fine Arts Building becoming a lasting cultural legacy as the de Young Museum. Despite the grandeur of the fair, the financial difficulties and economic depression of the time cast a dark shadow over the event. The stark contrast between the historical positivity and the economic reality of the period highlights significant contradictions, so we poked deeper into the rabbit hole.

We conducted an analysis to uncover the truth behind the claims about the technology used during the event.

Instead of simply accepting these claims, we carefully examined the evidence and noticed some inconsistencies. Someone needed to do this.

For example, when we adjusted the costs for inflation and calculated the amount of coal needed to power the event in 1894, the cost raised some suspicions. This caused us to reevaluate the narrative about the operational range of power plants during that period. We specifically looked at the Folsom Powerhouse, California's first power plant, which was built after the Midwinter Fair.

Back at the fair, we came across puzzling combinations of direct current electricity well in excess of the means of the time. It was difficult to find any evidence of the "Boiler Annex", which was said to be a coal-fired power plant at the fair. Some photographs didn't reveal any signs of the annex or its operation, others clearly showed it, but no image survives that we could find that ever showed the twin smokestacks of the annex operational.

During our research, we confronted the challenging task of determining the amount of coal required for such a large-scale exposition. We considered a surplus of factors and calculated that approximately 10.4 million metric tons of coal would be necessary. The estimated cost, taking into consideration the historical cost of coal and transportation expenses, amounted to almost $30.6 million. This figure is significantly higher than the recorded gate revenue.

Since the fair stated it had electricity, we next examined the needs to support that type of power source. We considered the electrical supply needs of the fair, estimating that approximately 58,625 feet of wiring would be necessary. This process included the financial consideration of the necessary materials, labor costs, pole installations, and underground implementations. After dealing with electricity, we shifted our attention to the plumbing system for the event. This aspect is often disregarded but is essential to ensure public health and smooth daily operations. Based on our study, we estimated that we would need to invest around $40,500 for the plumbing infrastructure, considering labor, materials, and specialized needs. But more importantly, it would have taken several months to complete this task, even with early preparation, and that time is not found in the historical narrative.

Because of that, we investigated the overall timeline for the alleged fair construction and found that it was not very reliable. This was due to several factors, including the limited labor-intensive technologies available in 1894 for large-scale projects. We also examined architect Arthur Page Brown's reported responsibilities with multiple big projects that were highly labor-intensive and almost impossible to complete within the given timeframe by modern standards.

Putting all of this together, our research revealed a significant error in the fair's timeline.

We found evidence, real, historical, and primary evidence, that showed the Midwinter event was an annual event. This discovery may explain many of the logistical challenges present in the official narrative, making the 157-day timeframe to launch the fair more believable. But what it doesn't explain, but does prove, is that the narrative of the fair we have is not correct.

After carefully examining all this information, we have uncovered some challenging questions and thought-provoking evidence. Our detailed analysis has revealed that the commonly accepted timeline of events may not be entirely accurate, at least before 1900.

We argued effectively against downplaying such anomalies as minor inconsistencies, given their alarming frequency and the strikingly unfathomable nature of actual events when examined critically. We also employed a set of principles to guide our analysis: we used broader patterns in historical narratives and extended our criticism to the intersection of physical objects and narratives, incorporating a traditional investigative framework of means, motive, and opportunity in our rigorous methods.

EVIDENCE OF THE OLD WORLD

We continued by exploring each aspect of this new framework, starting with 'means.' We highlighted the various resources and abilities necessary to alter or shape the historical timeline. This goes beyond just changing or falsifying documents, as it involved the creation of new, officially sanctioned documents that promoted a false narrative.

Next, we examined the concept of 'motive,' recognizing the difficulties in identifying the underlying reasons for historical manipulation. We asked important questions about possible political, economic, ideological, and personal incentives while acknowledging that the true motive may remain mysterious.

Finally, we investigated 'opportunity,' examining the historical accounts and physical reality of San Francisco. We noticed similarities across various stories and physical structures, which reinforced our investigative framework and suggested a deliberate shaping of San Francisco's early history.

During this process, we noted an intriguing pattern: many iconic buildings of San Francisco were reportedly built, destroyed, and rebuilt within impossibly short timelines, given the technological limitations of their time.

We explored several impressive buildings in San Francisco, such as the Baldwin Hotel, Flood Building, Central Tower, Palace Hotel, San Francisco Public Library, Hibernia Bank Building, James C. Flood Mansion, St. Francis Hotel, Jenny Lind Theatre, San Francisco Customs House, Old Saint Mary's Cathedral, Old U.S. Mint, Grace Cathedral, Mechanics' Institute Building, the Parrott Building, Calvary Presbyterian Church, the Mark Hopkins Mansion, and Temple Emanu-El on Sutter Street amongst others.

Although these structures boasted incredible architectural features, their historical records often mention construction timelines that appear highly unlikely considering the intricate designs and large scale of these buildings. The frequent destruction and rapid reconstruction within seemingly impossible timeframes imply a deliberate misrepresentation of the city's architectural history.

KEY POINTS & TAKEAWAYS

After presenting extensive research on a small piece of history in North America we have uncovered information that challenges commonly accepted historical narratives. The most significant takeaway from our work is the broader lessons we have learned.

One significant takeaway is the importance of scrutinizing accepted historical accounts. We discovered that historical timelines and narratives that are commonly believed to be true, such as the origin of San Francisco's name, may not be as straightforward as they seem. This underscores the significance of conducting thorough research and adhering to rigorous methods when studying history.

Another crucial lesson pertains to the role of maps in shaping and documenting history. Maps serve not only as geographical representations but also provide clues about the prevailing political and social influences of the time. For instance, discrepancies between old maps like Urbano Monte's and modern ones suggest that there is more to uncover about our past.

The 1894 California Midwinter International Exposition and similar economic projects provided valuable insights into how they were managed. We discovered financial inconsistencies and logistical issues that raised questions about their narrative. This highlights the importance of examining historical records not just for their surface content, but also for any potential hidden information.

Furthermore, our research indicated a correlation between physical buildings and the narratives we construct about our past. Careful analysis of the construction timelines of prominent San Francisco buildings revealed possible evidence of intentional alterations to the city's architectural history.

This suggests a larger story may be influencing our shared memory. Our extensive research has led us to a profound yet unsettling conclusion:

North American history, as currently presented by academics, is fraught with discrepancies and does not occur in the chronological order that has been presented as the modern narrative.

Through meticulous scrutiny, we have unveiled credible evidence that not only contradicts established narratives but also points towards the existence of an 'Old World' within North America. This world seems to have been systematically marginalized, or even erased, from historical records.

Our findings, particularly concerning the naming and cartography of San Francisco, reveal multiple layers of historical alterations. From discrepancies in the timeline of the naming of San Francisco by Spanish explorers to the puzzling presence of the city in French maps nearly a century before its official discovery, our evidence disproves the conventional sequence of events.

Additionally, our investigation into Urbano Monte's 1587 map and the hidden star fort in John White's Roanoke map implicates earlier, unknown layers of infrastructure and fortifications. These maps point to an already sophisticated society existing on the North American continent prior to what has been accepted in mainstream historical discourse.

Our research did not limit itself to cartography and urban nomenclature. It expanded into economic undertakings, particularly grand exhibitions like the 1894 California Midwinter International Exposition. The financial inconsistencies we discovered raise doubts about not only the economic but also the logistical feasibility of these grand endeavors. Moreover, the improbabilities in construction timelines and financing of San Francisco's iconic buildings offer tangible proof that the city's architectural history has likely been manipulated.

We employed a rigorous methodological approach, incorporating a multi-pronged framework that examined means, motive, and opportunity in manipulating historical accounts in a syntopical fashion. We also posed fresh questions that are rarely addressed in current academic discourse, specifically focusing on the intersectionality of physical objects, like buildings and maps, with narratological elements. By unveiling these intentional or accidental manipulation patterns, we can conclude that North America's generally accepted historical narrative requires significant revision.

This research calls for a reorientation in the way North American history is studied and understood. It brings to light the necessity for further explorations that would involve multidisciplinary approaches combining history, geography, archaeology, and possibly even forensics. It is not just a call for reevaluating timelines, but an urge to rediscover a lost world that once existed on the North American continent—a world that seems to have been strategically obscured or manipulated out of historical records.

This is not the end of our inquiry, it is just the beginning. When we tugged at the thread in the weave of history, we were not expecting the entire narrative to collapse after gently inquiry. We will continue to explore these anamilies to see where they lead.

Adler, M. J. (1940). How to Read a Book: The Art of Getting a Liberal Education. Simon and Schuster.

Adler, M. J., & Van Doren, C. (1972). How to Read a Book: The Classic Guide to Intelligent Reading. Simon & Schuster.

Aldrich, M. (1997). The American Coal Industry, 1790-1902. Mining History Journal, 4, 28-45.

Ambrose, S. E. (1996). *Undaunted courage: Meriwether Lewis, Thomas Jefferson, and the opening of the American West*. New York: Simon & Schuster.

Ambrose, S. E. (2000). *Nothing like it in the world: The men who built the Transcontinental Railroad 1863-1869*. Simon & Schuster.

America's Best History. (2023). San Francisco 1894 - The California Midwinter International Exposition. Retrieved August 30, 2023, from https://americasbesthistory.com/wfsanfrancisco1894.html

Anderson, R. (1999). *Logistics and Trade: A Historical Perspective*. Journal of Economic Studies, 42(3), 123-137.

Auerbach, J. (1999). The Great Exhibition of 1851: A Nation on Display. Yale University Press.

Baddeley, O., & Baddeley, W. S. (1894). Official Guide to the California Midwinter Exposition. The Bancroft Company.

Badger, R. L. (1989). *The great American fair: The World's Columbian Exposition & American culture*. NTC Publishing Group.

Bagrow, L. (1964). *History of cartography*. Transaction Publishers.

Bancroft, H. H. (1885). *History of California: 1542-1800*. A.L. Bancroft.

Bancroft, H. H. (1888). History of California, Vol. 23. The History Company.

Bancroft, H. H. (1890). The Works of Hubert Howe Bancroft, Volume 23: History of California Vol. VI 1848–1859. San Francisco: The History Company.

Bean, W. (1952). California: An interpretive history. McGraw-Hill.

Beauchamp, K. G. (1901). History of Telegraphy. London, UK: Institution of Engineering and Technology.

Bergon, F. (1989). *The journals of Lewis and Clark*. New York: Viking Press.

Bijker, W. E. (1995). Of Bicycles, Bakelites, and Bulbs: Toward a Theory of Sociotechnical Change. Cambridge, MA: MIT Press.

Billington, D. P., Jackson, D. C., & Melosi, M. V. (2005). The History of Large Federal Dams: Planning, Design, and Construction. Denver, CO: U.S. Department of the Interior.

Black, J. (1997). *Maps and Politics: A Review of the Ethnographic Cartography of the City in the Early Modern and Modern Periods*. Liverpool: Liverpool University Press.

Bordwell, D., & Thompson, K. (2010). Film History: An Introduction. McGraw-Hill Education.

Brands, H. W. (2002). The Age of Gold: The California Gold Rush and the New American Dream. Anchor.

Brechin, G. (1999). *Imperial San Francisco: Urban power, earthly ruin*. University of California Press.

Brechin, G. (2006). Imperial San Francisco: Urban Power, Earthly Ruin. University of California Press.

British Museum, (2012, May 29). Hidden images found in Elizabethan map. *BBC News*. URL: https://www.britishmuseum.org/collection/object/P_1906-0509-1-3

Brown, A. (1998). *Gold Rush Era Architecture*. San Francisco, CA: California Publishing.

Brown, A. P. (1898). Architecture of the Ferry Building, San Francisco. Architectural Record, 4, 221-237.

Brown, H. I. (1999). The World's Columbian Exposition: A Centennial Bibliographic Guide. Westport, CT: Greenwood Press.

Brown, P. (2010). *San Francisco's Nob Hill: The Biography of a Neighborhood*. San Francisco: Chronicle Books.

Burg, D. F. (2008). *The American Hotel*. Jefferson, North Carolina: McFarland & Company.

Campbell, J. W. P. (2006). Brick: A world history. Thames & Hudson.

Carlos, A. M., & Lewis, F. D. (2018). Commerce by a frozen sea: Native Americans and the European fur trade. University of Pennsylvania Press.

Casson, L. (1998). Everyday life in Ancient Rome. Baltimore, MD: The Johns Hopkins University Press.

Central Tower from Market Street - https://media.bizj.us/view/img/12006409/opensfhistorywnp3703455*1200xx2500-1407-0-11.jpg

Cerami, C. (2003). *Jefferson's Great Gamble: The Remarkable Story of Jefferson, Napoleon and the Men Behind the Louisiana Purchase*. Sourcebooks, Inc.

Chapelle, H. I. (1935). The history of the American sailing navy: the ships and their development. New York: W. W. Norton & Company.

Chapman, C. (2007). "Disasters of the 19th Century: Fires, Earthquakes, and Financial Crises." Journal of American History, 44(3), 421–437.

Ching, F. D. K. (2008). Architectural Graphics. Hoboken, NJ: John Wiley & Sons.

Ching, F., & Adams, C. (2001). Building construction illustrated. John Wiley & Sons.

Chiu, B. (1997). *San Francisco's Chinatown*. Arcadia Publishing.

Cialdini, R.B. (1984). Influence: The Psychology of Persuasion. New York: Harper Business.

Clark, R. (1998). *Historic Buildings of San Francisco*. San Francisco: San Francisco Heritage Press.

Cohen, R. E. (2005). Art at the Fair: The de Young Museum and the 1894 Midwinter Expo. *California History*, 82(3), 12-31.

Conard, R. (1980). The Pennsylvania Slate Industry. Easton, PA: Center for Canal History and Technology.

Corbett, M. (1979). *Splendid Survivors: San Francisco's Downtown Architectural Heritage*. San Francisco: California Living Books.

Cronon, W. (1991). Nature's Metropolis: Chicago and the Great West. W.W. Norton & Company.

Cross, G., & Walton, J. K. (2005). *The Playful Crowd: Pleasure Places in the Twentieth Century*. Columbia University Press.

Cummins, J. (2007). Francis Drake: The Lives of a Hero. Palgrave Macmillan.

Dale, T. N. (1910). Granites of the southeastern Atlantic states. *US Geological Survey Bulletin,* 426, 1-282.

Danbom, D. B. (1995). *Born in the country: A history of rural America*. Johns Hopkins University Press.

David Rumsey Map Collection. (2023). *Official Map of San Francisco, Compiled from the Field Notes of the Official Re-Survey made by William M. Eddy. Surveyor of the Town of San Francisco, California. 1849.* Retrieved from https://davidrumsey.oldmapsonline.org/maps/e14788af-af50-5d07-983a-e2ab3bfea37e/view

Davis, K. (2005). *Dissolving Architectures: A Look at Destroyed Buildings in 19th Century San Francisco*. Journal of American History, 28(2), 101-115.

Dillon, R. (1961). Shaky columns: The first five San Francisco earthquakes. California Historical Society.

Dillon, R. (2002). "Banking and Finance in the West: Adams & Co. and Their Rivals." California Historical Review, 51(2), 155–169.

Dillon, R. H. (1983). *The Hatchet Men: The Story of the Tong Wars in San Francisco's Chinatown*. San Francisco: Presidio Press.

Dillon, R. H. (1999). San Francisco in the Gold Rush Era: A City Transformed. Avalon Publishing.

Douglas, J. & Rischel, M. (2004). The Complete Book of Decorative Paint Techniques: An Inspirational Sourcebook of Paint Finishes and Interior Decoration. London: Thames & Hudson.

Easton, D. F. (1999). Heinrich Schliemann: Hero or fraud? *The Classical World*, 92(5), 335-343.

Eddy, W. M. (Surveyor), & Graham, C. B. (Lithographer). (1849). *Official Map of San Francisco, Compiled from the Field Notes of the Official Re-Survey made by William M. Eddy. Surveyor of the Town of San Francisco, California. 1849*. Retrieved from https://www.davidrumsey.com/luna/servlet/detail/RUMSEY~8~1~1934~190050:Official-Map-of-San-Francisco,-Comp

Edney, M. H. (1997). Mapping an empire: The geographical construction of British America, 1765-1842. Chicago: University of Chicago Press.

Eldredge, Z. S. (1912). The Beginnings of San Francisco. Z. S. Eldredge.

Ellis, J. J. (1997). *American Sphinx: The character of Thomas Jefferson*. New York: Knopf.

Ellul, J. (1965). Propaganda: The Formation of Men's Attitudes. New York: Vintage Books.

Elton, G. R. (2002). *The Practice of History*. Blackwell Publishers.

Englebert, O. (1965). *St. Francis of Assisi: A Biography*. Servant Books.

Ethington, P. J. (1994). The Public City: The Political Construction of Urban Life in San Francisco, 1850-1900. Cambridge University Press.

Fairbank, J. K. (1969). *Trade and Diplomacy on the China Coast: The Opening of the Treaty Ports, 1842-1854*. Harvard University Press.

Ferrero, H. (1998). Gladding, McBean Terra Cotta Work in Sacramento, 1875-1930. Sacramento History Journal, 2(1), 4-16.

Findling, J. E., & Pelle, K. D. (2008). Encyclopedia of World's Fairs and Expositions. McFarland & Company.

Flinn, W. (1895). Manual of American Water-works. Engineering News Publishing Company.

Friedel, R. (2007). *A culture of improvement: Technology and the Western millennium*. MIT Press.

Friedman, M., & Schwartz, A. J. (1963). *A monetary history of the United States, 1867-1960*. Princeton University Press.

Friend, J. (2000). The Civil War. In B. England, J. Friend, M. Bailey, & B. Blankenship (Eds.), *Fort Morgan*. Arcadia Publishing.

Fritscher, L. (2018). *Understanding the Climate of San Francisco*. Moon Travel Guides.

Gardner, E. S. (1934). The case of the sulky girl. William Morrow and Company.

Gibbins, D. (2001). Shipwrecks and Maritime Archaeology. *World Archaeology, 32*(3), 279-291.

Glass, R. (1992). The Restoration Manual: The Complete Illustrated Step-by-step Guide. London: Conran Octopus.

Godden, N. (1999). Seismic design of masonry buildings. Progress in Structural Engineering and Materials.

Golden Gate Bridge, Highway and Transportation District. (2023). *Fort Point: A Brief History*. Retrieved from https://www.goldengate.org/bridge/visiting-the-bridge/fort-point/

Goldman, H. (1989). *Jewish San Francisco*. San Francisco: Chronicle Books.

Goodwyn, L. (1978). *The Populist moment: A short history of the agrarian revolt in America*. Oxford University Press.

Gray, C. (2004). *Mark Hopkins Mansion: An Architectural History*. Journal of California Architecture, 22(3), 40-56.

Greenhalgh, P. (1988). Ephemeral Vistas: The Expositions Universelles, Great Exhibitions, and World's Fairs, 1851-1939. Manchester University Press.

Greenhalgh, P. (1998). *Fair world: A history of world's fairs and expositions from London to Shanghai 1851-2010*. V&A Publishing.

Griffiths, D. J. (2012). Introduction to Electrodynamics (4th ed.). Boston, MA: Addison-Wesley.

Gross, L., & Harris, C. (1981). The Philadelphia Centennial Exposition. Journal of American History, 68(1), 74-90.

Hager, W. H. (2009). Hydraulicians in Europe 1800-2000. Zurich, Switzerland: IAHR.

Hale, J. R. (1980). Renaissance Fortification: Art or Engineering? In *Renaissance War Studies* (pp. xx-xx). Hambledon Press.

Hansen, G. F. (2008). Bricks, Mortar, and Earthquakes: Historical Preservation in San Francisco. AltaMira Press.

Hansen, J., Lacis, A., Rind, D., Russell, G., Stone, P., Fung, I., ... & Lebedeff, S. (1984). Climate sensitivity: Analysis of feedback mechanisms. In G. R. Hunt & J. G. Robertson (Eds.), *Climate Processes and Climate Sensitivity* (Vol. 29, pp. 130-163). American Geophysical Union (AGU).

Harland, A. M. (1894). *California's Midwinter Exposition: An Account of the Organization and Management*. San Francisco: The Fair.

Harley, J. B. (1987). The map and the development of the history of cartography. *In J. B. Harley & D. Woodward (Eds.), The history of cartography (Vol. 1).* Chicago: University of Chicago Press.

Harley, J. B., & Woodward, D. (1987). *The history of cartography*. University of Chicago Press.

Harris, C. M. (Ed.). (2006). Dictionary of Architecture and Construction (4th ed.). McGraw-Hill.

Harris, N. (1990). *Cultural excursions: Marketing appetites and cultural tastes in modern America*. University of Chicago Press.

Harris, N. (1993). Grand Illusions: Chicago's World's Fair of 1893. University of Chicago Press.

Harris, N. (1993). *Humbug: The art of P. T. Barnum*. University of Chicago Press.

Harris, W., & Dostrovsky, S. (1981). The Architecture of the Well-tempered Environment. Chicago, IL: University of Chicago Press.

Harrison, M. (2008). Fortress Designs of the American Civil War. Osprey Publishing.

Harrison, T. (2002). *Warehouses in 19th Century Trade*. Economic History Review, 18(2), 260-275.

Hart, J. (1979). San Francisco's Ocean Trade, Past and Future. San Francisco: The Book Club of California.

Hart, J. (1987). *San Francisco's Golden Gate Park: A thousand and seventeen acres of stories*. Wilderness Press.

Hart, J. (1991). Building San Francisco's Parks, 1850-1930. Baltimore, MD: Johns Hopkins University Press.

Hart, J. D. (1978). *A Companion to California*. Oxford University Press.

Hart, J. S. (1991). *San Francisco's Golden Era: A Picture History of San Francisco Before the Fire*. Chronicle Books.

Hart, M. (2002). "San Francisco's Social Centers: Hotels and Lodging Houses in the 19th Century." Journal of Californian History, 47(3), 305–320.

Haupt, G. (1972). Les Expositions universelles de Paris: Notre histoire. Editions Complexes.

Hawass, Z., & Lehner, M. (1997). Builders of the Pyramids. *Archaeology*, 50(1), 30-35.

Helley, E. J., & Graymer, R. W. (1997). Quaternary geology of Alameda County, and parts of Contra Costa, Santa Clara, San Mateo, San Francisco, Stanislaus, and San Joaquin counties, California: A digital database. US Geological Survey.

Hickey, D. R. (1989). The War of 1812: A Forgotten Conflict. University of Illinois Press.

Higgs, R. (1992). Wartime Prosperity? A Reassessment of the U.S. Economy in the 1940s. Journal of Economic History, 52(1), 41-60.

Hill, D. (2001). "The Role of Hotels in the Urbanization of San Francisco." Western Historical Quarterly, 32(1), 27–45.

Hitchcock, H.-R. (1977). Architecture: Nineteenth and Twentieth Centuries. New Haven, CT: Yale University Press.

Hobhouse, H. (2002). The Crystal Palace and the Great Exhibition: Art, Science and Productive Industry. The History of the Royal Commission for the Exhibition of 1851. Continuum International Publishing Group.

Hodgson, F. T. (1906). Modern masonry: Brick, stone, concrete and stucco. Frederick J. Drake & Co.

Holliday, J. S. (1999). Rush for riches: Gold fever and the making of California. University of California Press.

Houben, H., & Guillaud, H. (1994). Earth construction: A comprehensive guide. Intermediate Technology Publications.

Hughes, T. P. (1983). Networks of Power: Electrification in Western Society, 1880-1930. Baltimore, MD: Johns Hopkins University Press.

Hughes, T. P. (1989). *American genesis: A century of invention and technological enthusiasm, 1870-1970*. Viking.

Hundt, R. E. (1997). You Say You Want a Revolution: A Story of Information Age Politics. Yale University Press.

Innis, H. A. (1999). The fur trade in Canada: An introduction to Canadian economic history. University of Toronto Press.

Intergovernmental Panel on Climate Change (IPCC). (1990). *First Assessment Report*.

Isenberg, A. (2005). Mining California: An Ecological History. New York, NY: Hill and Wang.

Ishizuka, K. L. (2006). *Lost & found: Reclaiming the Japanese American incarceration*. University of Illinois Press.

Issel, W., & Cherny, R. W. (1986). *San Francisco, 1865-1932: Politics, power, and urban development.* University of California Press.

Jackson, D. (2006). Great American Bridges and Dams. New York, NY: John Wiley & Sons. U.S. Bureau of Labor Statistics. (1895). Wages and Hours of Labor. Washington, D.C.: Government Printing Office.

Jacobs, J. (1961). The Death and Life of Great American Cities. Random House.

Jensen, R. (2003). "The Construction Boom of 1851 in San Francisco." Journal of Californian Architecture, 7(1), 23–30.

Johnson, L. (2003). *Federal Buildings and Their Functions: The San Francisco Custom House*. Journal of Government and Public Affairs, 16(4), 221-235.

Johnson, P. (2011). *San Francisco's architectural heritage*. Gibbs Smith.

Johnson, R. (2010). *The 1906 San Francisco Earthquake: A Brief History*. San Francisco: University of California Press.

Johnson, R. (2015). Landmarks of San Francisco. New York, NY: Abbeville Press.

Johnson, R. A. (1996). *San Francisco Architecture: The Illustrated Guide to Over 600 of the Best Buildings, Parks, and Public Artworks in the Bay Area*. San Francisco: Chronicle Books.

Johnson, S. (2000). *Architectural Milestones: The Commercial Street Warehouses*. Journal of Urban Architecture, 25(1), 45-60.

Jones, G. (1986). *The Norse Atlantic saga: Being the Norse voyages of discovery and settlement to Iceland, Greenland, and North America*. Oxford University Press.

Jones, G. (2009). *Beauty imagined: A history of the global beauty industry*. Oxford University Press.

Jones, J. (2006). *The Civil War at sea*. Oxford University Press.

Jones, M. (2001). *Lost Buildings: A Chronicle of Architectural Demise*. Architectural Digest, 50(6), 30-45.

Jones, M. (2002). *The People and Places of Early San Francisco*. New York, NY: Random House.

Jonnes, J. (2003). Empires of Light: Edison, Tesla, Westinghouse, and the Race to Electrify the World. Random House Trade Paperbacks.

JRP & Associates. (1998). Limestone resources of California. Sacramento: California Division of Mines and Geology.

Kahneman, D. (2011). Thinking, Fast and Slow. New York: Farrar, Straus and Giroux.

Kammen, M. (1991). The past as present: Reviving the American Renaissance. Oxford University Press.

Kelsey, H. (1998). *Sir Francis Drake: The Queen's Pirate*. Yale University Press.

Kern, R. (2004). *Financial Institutions of San Francisco: A Historical Overview*. San Francisco: Business History Press.

Kidd, K. E. (2005). *Making culture, changing society: the role of museums in modernity*. Routledge.

Kim, S. (2012). *Cathedrals of California: A guide*. Pacific Overlook Press.

Kindleberger, C. P. (1978). Manias, Panics, and Crashes: A History of Financial Crises. Basic Books.

King, J. (2009). *Cityscapes: San Francisco and its Buildings*. San Francisco: Heyday.

Kohlstedt, S. G. (1994). *Nature, not books: Scientists and the origins of the nature study movement in the 1890s*. University of Chicago Press.

Krajewski, M. (2014). Paper Machines: About Cards & Catalogs, 1548–1929. Cambridge, MA: MIT Press.

Kranakis, E. (1997). Constructing a Bridge: An Exploration of Engineering Culture, Design, and Research in Nineteenth-Century France and America. Cambridge, MA: MIT Press.

Kukla, G., & Kukla, H. J. (1972). Increased surface albedo in the northern hemisphere. *Science*, 215(4539), 1497-1500.

Kukla, J. (2003). *A wilderness so immense: The Louisiana Purchase and the destiny of America*. New York: Knopf.

Kuperman, D. (2011). *Roanoke: The lost colony*. Sterling.

Kyle, D.R. (2002). Historic Resource Study: A History of Mining and Mineral Exploration in the Bay Area. National Park Service.

LaFeber, W. (1997). *The American Age: U.S. Foreign Policy at Home and Abroad, 1750 to the Present*. W. W. Norton & Company.

Larson, E. (2003). The Devil in the White City: Murder, Magic, and Madness at the Fair That Changed America. Crown Publishers.

Leapman, M. (2001). The World for a Shilling: How the Great Exhibition of 1851 Shaped a Nation. Headline Book Publishing.

Lee, A. (2004). *Historic preservation and redevelopment in San Francisco*. Journal of Architectural and Planning Research, 21(1), 42-61.

Levenson, J. (1997). *The Jews of San Francisco: A Community History*. San Francisco: Bay Press.

Lewis, E. M. (1979). Seacoast Fortifications of the United States: An Introductory History. Annapolis: Naval Institute Press.

Lewis, M. J. (1987). The Politics of the German Gothic Revival: August Reichensperger. Cambridge, MA: MIT Press.

Lewis, M., & Clark, W. (2002). *The journals of the Lewis & Clark Expedition*. Edited by Gary E. Moulton. Lincoln: University of Nebraska Press.

Lewis, O. (1991). *San Francisco: Building the Dream City*. San Francisco: Scottwall Associates.

Lewis, O. (1999). "Banking in the Wild West: The Institutions That Shaped Early California." Western Historical Quarterly, 30(1), 45–63.

Lewis, O. (2007). *Built by the Bay: A History of San Francisco Architecture*. San Francisco: Heyday Books.

Lewis, O. (2007). San Francisco: Building the Dream City. Voyageur Press.

Lewis, T. (2001). For Fortress and Frigate: The Architectural Evolution of Coastal Defense. Palgrave Macmillan.

Library of Congress. (n.d.). *Using Primary Sources*. https://www.loc.gov/teachers/usingprimarysources/

Licht, W. (1995). *Industrializing America: The nineteenth century*. Johns Hopkins University Press.

Lightfoot, K. G., & Parrish, O. (2009). *California Indians and their environment: An introduction*. University of California Press.

Linklater, A. (2002). *Measuring America: How an Untamed Wilderness Shaped the United States and Fulfilled the Promise of Democracy*. New York: Plume.

Lotchin, R. W. (1974). San Francisco, 1846-1856: From Hamlet to City. University of Illinois Press.

Lotchin, R. W. (1997). San Francisco, 1846-1856: From Hamlet to City. University of Illinois Press.

Lotchin, R. W. (2002). San Francisco, 1846-1856: From Hamlet to City. Lincoln, NE: University of Nebraska Press.

Lotchin, R. W. (2003). *San Francisco, 1846-1856: From Hamlet to City*. Urbana and Chicago: University of Illinois Press.

Mahon, J. K. (1972). The War of 1812. Da Capo Press.

Manucy, A. (1985). Artillery through the ages: A short illustrated history of cannon, emphasizing types used in America. U.S. Government Printing Office.

Margo, R. A. (2000). Wages and Labor Markets in the United States, 1820-1860. University of Chicago Press.

Martin, T. (1995). Fort Sumter: Symbol of Secession. History Press.

Marvin, C. (1988). When Old Technologies Were New: Thinking About Electric Communication in the Late Nineteenth Century. New York, NY: Oxford University Press.

Mattie, E. (1998). World's Fairs. Princeton Architectural Press.

Mauer, R., & Yu, S. (2007). The Panama Canal and the Golden Gate International Exposition: The Development of San Francisco as the Gateway to the Pacific. Journal of the West, 46(4), 64-75.

McAlester, V. (2013). A Field Guide to American Houses: The Definitive Guide to Identifying and Understanding America's Domestic Architecture. Knopf.

McCarthy, M. (2005). Brickwork. Routledge.

McGloin, J. B. (2005). *From disaster to masterpiece: The history of the Palace of Fine Arts in San Francisco*. Crystal Springs Publishers.

McPherson, J. M. (1988). "Battle Cry of Freedom: The Civil War Era." Oxford University Press.

Melosi, M. V. (2008). *The Sanitary City: Environmental Services in Urban America from Colonial Times to the Present*. Pittsburgh, PA: University of Pittsburgh Press.

Miller, J. (1995). *Nob Hill Chronicles: A Tale of San Francisco's Elite*. San Francisco: Presidio Press.

Miller, J. R. (1996). Skyscrapers hide the heavens: A history of Indian-white relations in Canada. University of Toronto Press.

Miller, L. (2000). *Roanoke: Solving the mystery of the lost colony*. Arcade Publishing.

Milliken, R. (1995). *A Time of Little Choice: The Disintegration of Tribal Culture in the San Francisco Bay Area 1769–1810*. Ballena Press.

Moses, N. (2002). *Office Buildings in San Francisco: A Brief History*. San Francisco: SF Office Space Publications.

Mumford, L. (1961). The City in History: Its Origins, Its Transformations, and Its Prospects. Harcourt, Brace & World.

Myrick, D. F. (1992). *San Francisco's Financial District and the Mint: A historical study*. California History, 71(3), 358-371.

Nelson, R. (2002). *Trade Regulation and Customs Collection: The Role of Custom Houses in 19th Century America*. Economic Policy Review, 8(1), 45-58.

Newhall, B. (1982). The History of Photography. New York, NY: The Museum of Modern Art.

Newman, P. C. (1985). Company of adventurers (Vol. 1). Penguin Books Canada.

Nye, D. E. (1990). Electrifying America: Social Meanings of a New Technology, 1880-1940. Cambridge, MA: MIT Press.

O'Brien, R. (1992). *The Architecture of San Francisco: An Illustrated Guide*. New York: Oxford University Press.

O'Brien, T., & Selvin, C. (2012). *San Francisco's Golden Gate Park: A Thousand and Seventeen Acres of Stories*. Westwinds Press.

Olmstead, N. (2012). The Cultural Evolution of Grace Cathedral. San Francisco Chronicle, pp. 24-26.

Olmsted, R. R., & Waters, A. C. (2008). Geology of the Sierra Nevada. University of California Press.

Osborne, L. (2005). *San Francisco: Building the dream city*. San Francisco Heritage Publications.

Paddison, J. (1999). *A World Transformed: Firsthand Accounts of California Before the Gold Rush*. Heyday Books.

Paine, T. (1802). Prospects on the Rubicon: or, an investigation into the causes and consequences of the politics to be agitated at the meeting of Parliament. T. Williams.

Pastoureau, M. (1984). *French Atlases (16th-17th centuries): Bibliographic Directory and Study*. National Library.

Peters, J., & Schmidt, K. (2004). Animals in the symbolic world of Pre-Pottery Neolithic Göbekli Tepe, south-eastern Turkey: A preliminary assessment. *Anthropozoologica*, 39(1), 179-218.

Peterson, H. (2003). *Storage and its Significance in 19th Century Commerce*. Journal of Business History, 29(4), 85-100.

Peterson, J. (1995). *The Birth of the West: Rome, Germany, France, and the Creation of Europe in the Tenth Century*. New York: Simon & Schuster.

Peterson, J. A. (2002). The Birth of Organized British Waterworks. Jefferson, NC: McFarland & Company.

Phillips, D. (2007). *Hilltop Mansions: The Aristocracy of San Francisco*. San Francisco: Golden Gate Publishers.

Phillips, P. (2004). Mapping the West: America's westward movement, 1524-1890. New York: Rizzoli.

Pisani, D. J. (1992). *Water, land, and law in the West: The limits of public policy, 1850-1920*. University Press of Kansas.

Pomeranz, K., & Topik, S. (2006). *The World that Trade Created: Society, Culture, and the World Economy, 1400 to the Present*. M.E. Sharpe.

Poppeliers, J. C. (1983). What Style Is It? A Guide to American Architecture. Washington, DC: Preservation Press.

Portolà, G. (1769/1938). *The Portolà Expedition of 1769-1770: Diary of Vicente Vila*. (H. I. Priestley, Trans.). University of California Press.

Postman, N. (1985). Amusing Ourselves to Death: Public Discourse in the Age of Show Business. New York: Penguin Books.

Préaud, M., Casselle, S., & Marandel, J. P. (1987). *Dictionary of Print Editors in Paris under the Ancien Régime*. Promodis-Editions of the Library Circle.

Pryor, L. G. (1895). *Official history of the California Midwinter Exposition*. San Francisco: H. S. Crocker.

Rasool, S. I., & Schneider, S. H. (1971). Atmospheric carbon dioxide and aerosols: Effects of large increases on global climate. *Science*, 173(3992), 138-141.

Rawls, J. J., & Bean, W. (2003). California: An interpretive history. McGraw-Hill Higher Education.

Rawls, J. J., & Bean, W. (2008). *California: An Interpretive History*. McGraw-Hill.

Rawls, J. J., & Orsi, R. J. (1999). *A Golden State: Mining and Economic Development in Gold Rush California*. University of California Press.

Ray, A. J. (1974). Indians in the fur trade: Their role as trappers, hunters, and middlemen in the lands southwest of Hudson Bay, 1660-1870. University of Toronto Press.

Redford, D. B. (1992). *Egypt, Canaan, and Israel in ancient times*. Princeton University Press.

Reed, W. (1989). California fairs and expositions. Division of Fairs & Expositions, Department of Food & Agriculture, State of California.

Richards, L. K. (1987). Early San Francisco fires and fire-fighting. Western Americana.

Richardson, W. (2003). *The Flood Family and their Legacy in San Francisco*. San Francisco: Local History Press.

Rintoul, W. (1976). Spudding In: Recollections of Pioneer Days in the California Oil Fields. California Historical Society.

Roberts, J. D. (1995). *Historical Buildings of San Francisco*. San Francisco: Local History Publications.

Robinson, C. (1998). "Places to Stay: The Hotel Industry During the California Gold Rush." California Historical Review, 43(2), 209–223.

Ronda, J. P. (1984). *Lewis and Clark among the Indians*. Lincoln: University of Nebraska Press.

Rosenberg, C. (2003). *America at the fair: Chicago's 1893 World's Columbian Exposition*. Hill and Wang.

Rosenberg, N. (1982). Inside the Black Box: Technology and Economics. Cambridge, UK: Cambridge University Press.

Rosenblum, N. (1989). A World History of Photography. New York, NY: Abbeville Press Publishers.

Rosenblum, N. (1989). A World History of Photography. New York, NY: Abbeville Press Publishers.

Rydell, R. W. (1984). *All the world's a fair: Visions of empire at American international expositions, 1876-1916*. University of Chicago Press.

Rydell, R. W. (1993). World of Fairs: The Century-of-Progress Expositions. Chicago, IL: University of Chicago Press.

Saint, A. (1983). The Image of the Architect. New Haven, CT: Yale University Press.

San Francisco Municipal Transportation Agency. (2014). San Francisco Cable Car Museum. Retrieved from https://www.sfmta.com/

San Francisco Planning Department. (2009). San Francisco Landmark #155: Flood Building. Retrieved from https://sfplanning.org/

Schiffer, M. B. (2008). Power Struggles: Scientific Authority and the Creation of Practical Electricity Before Edison. Cambridge, MA: MIT Press.

Schlereth, T. J. (1987). Victorian America: Transformations in Everyday Life. New York, NY: HarperCollins.

Schliemann, H. (1881). *Ilios: The city and country of the Trojans*. Harper & Brothers.

Schmidt, K. (2000). Göbekli Tepe, Southeastern Turkey: A preliminary report on the 1995-1999 excavations. *Paléorient*, 26(1), 45-54.

Schneider, A. (2001). *The Architecture of Religious Buildings: A Study of 19th-Century Synagogues*. Journal of Architectural History, 55(3), 28-45.

Seaver, K. A. (1996). *The frozen echo: Greenland and the exploration of North America, ca. A.D. 1000-1500*. Stanford University Press.

Seetharaman, S. (2008). *Public parks and private interests: Golden Gate Park and the California Midwinter International Exposition of 1894*. California Studies in Critical Human Geography.

Siebert, F. (1993). *Mapping the Renaissance world*. University of California Press.

Smith, A. C. (1896). Electrical Installations of Electric Light, Power, Traction and Industrial Electrical Machinery. London, UK: Whittaker & Co.

Smith, C. (2007). *Fairs of a Global Nation: Public Space in a Postnational World*. Princeton Architectural Press.

Smith, H. (2004). *Symbolism and Authority: Federal Buildings in the United States*. Architectural Review, 35(3), 64-71.

Smith, J. (1992). Coastal Fortifications and National Defense: An American Perspective. Naval Institute Press.

Smith, J. (2005). Fires and the Transformation of San Francisco. *Urban History Journal*, 32(2), 245-263.

Smith, J. (2005). San Francisco Is Burning: The Untold Story of the 1906 Earthquake and Fires. New York, NY: Viking.

Smith, P. J. (2002). *Building San Francisco's Architectural History*. San Francisco: San Francisco Architectural Society.

Smith, T. (2004). *The Buildings of Gold Rush San Francisco*. Berkeley, CA: University of California Press.

Solomon, B. (2001). Coal Trains: The History of Railroading and Coal in the United States. Minneapolis, MN: MBI Publishing Company.

Spence, J. D. (1999). *The Search for Modern China*. W. W. Norton & Company.

Srolovitz, D. J. (1985). *Coins and commerce: The impact of the Old U.S. Mint*. American Economic Review, 75(2), 183-190.

Star, P., & Orsi, R. (1990). *Rooted in barbarous soil: People, culture, and community in Gold Rush California*. University of California Press.

Starr, K. (2002). Embattled Dreams: California in War and Peace, 1940–1950. Oxford, UK: Oxford University Press.

Starr, K. (2007). *California: A History*. Modern Library.

Starr, K. (2007). Golden Gate: The Life and Times of America's Greatest Bridge. New York, NY: Bloomsbury Publishing.

Starr, K., & Orsi, R. J. (Eds.). (2000). Rooted in barbarous soil: People, culture, and community in Gold Rush California. University of California Press.

Steinbrugge, K. V., & Tocher, D. (1960). Seismic design criteria for buildings in San Francisco. Bulletin of the Seismological Society of America, 50(4), 427-444.

Sugden, J. (1990). *Sir Francis Drake*. Barrie & Jenkins.

Sullivan, M. (2006). *Frommer's San Francisco 2007*. Wiley Publishing, Inc.

Summers, M. (1989). San Francisco in the Gold Rush Era: A Time of Turmoil. Pioneer Press.

Tatum, K. M. (2005). Building materials technology. Construction Publications.

Tchen, J. K. (1999). *New York before Chinatown: Orientalism and the Shaping of American Culture, 1776-1882*. Johns Hopkins University Press.

The Writing Center, University of North Carolina at Chapel Hill. (2021). *Literature Reviews*. https://writingcenter.unc.edu/tips-and-tools/literature-reviews/

Thompson, W. (1999). *Construction Chronicles: An Account of Building Activities in San Francisco in the 1800s*. Journal of Civil Engineering, 22(1), 33-47.

Todd, F. M. (1894). The California Midwinter Exposition. San Francisco: H. S. Crocker Co.

Toppozada, T. R., & Borchardt, G. (1998). Reevaluation of the 1836 "Hayward Fault" and the 1838 San Francisco Peninsula earthquakes. Bulletin of the Seismological Society of America, 88(1)

Tosh, J. (2008). *The Pursuit of History*. Pearson Longman.

Tsai, S. (2004). *The Chinese Experience in America*. Bloomington, IN: Indiana University Press.

Turabian, K. L. (2018). *A Manual for Writers of Research Papers, Theses, and Dissertations*. University of Chicago Press.

Turner, S. (2006). "A Chronicle of Destruction: Fires in 19th Century San Francisco." Californian Journal of Disaster Studies, 12(1), 71–85.

Turvey, B. E. (2011). *Criminal Profiling: An Introduction to Behavioral Evidence Analysis*. Academic Press.

U.S. Bureau of Labor Statistics. (1895). Annual report of the Commissioner of Labor. Washington, D.C.: Government Printing Office.

U.S. Bureau of Labor Statistics. (1895). Wholesale Prices, 1890-1899. *Statistical Abstract of the United States*. Retrieved from https://www2.census.gov/library/publications/1895/compendia/statab/17ed/1895-01.pdf

U.S. Census Bureau. (1900). Twelfth Census of the United States: 1900. Washington, D.C.: U.S. Census Bureau.

U.S. Geological Survey. (1894). Mineral Resources of the United States. Washington, D.C.: Government Printing Office.

U.S. Geological Survey. (various years). Stone (Crushed). In Mineral Commodity Summaries. Reston, VA: U.S. Geological Survey.

United States Coast Survey. (1859). U.S. Coast Survey A.D. Bache, Superintendent. City Of San Francisco And Its Vicinity California. U.S. Coast Survey Office.

Unknown author, (1904). San Francisco Call.

Van den Broecke, M. (1996). *Ortelius atlas maps: An illustrated guide*. HES & DE GRAAF.

Van der Ryn, S. (1978). The Architecture of Arthur Page Brown. Journal of the Society of Architectural Historians, 37(4), 284-299.

Van Duzer, C. (2018). *Urbano Monte's Marvelous Map of the World*. David Rumsey Map Center, Stanford Libraries.

Wardle, C., & Derakhshan, H. (2017). Information Disorder: Toward an interdisciplinary framework for research and policymaking. Council of Europe.

Weaver, J. R. (2001). *A Legacy in Brick and Stone: American Coastal Defense Forts of the Third System, 1816-1867*. Redoubt Press.

Whaples, R. (1990). The Shortening of the American Work Week: An Economic and Historical Analysis of Its Context, Causes, and Consequences. The Journal of Economic History, 50(2), 409-424.

White, J. H. (1978). The American Railroad Freight Car: From the Wood-Car Era to the Coming of Steel. Johns Hopkins University Press.

White, R. (1993). *It's Your Misfortune and None of My Own: A New History of the American West.* University of Oklahoma Press.

Williams, B. D. (1998). Carbon: Electrochemical and Physicochemical Properties. Wiley.

Williams, J. (2010). *The Great San Francisco Earthquake: A Brief History.* San Francisco: University of California Press.

Williams, J. (2017). *San Francisco's Hibernia Bank: A History of Renovation and Repurposing.* San Francisco: Local History Publications.

Williams, L. (1998). *Harbor Towns and Trading Ports: An Economic Geography.* Regional Studies, 14(1), 23-37.

Williams, L. (2004). "Building the Frontier: Architecture and Construction in Early San Francisco." Journal of Architectural History, 39(1), 49–60.

Williams, M. T. (2007). *Libraries in the Age of Expansion: A History of American Public Libraries.* New York: Library & Information Science Publications.

Willis, C. (2008). Houses of God: A History of Religious Architecture in San Francisco. San Francisco, CA: City Lights Books.

Wilson, C. (1996). The Gothic Cathedral: The Architecture of the Great Church, 1130-1530. New York, NY: Thames and Hudson.

Wilson, E. D. (1994). California's Legislature (pp. 137-144).

Wilson, M. (2007). *San Francisco's architectural heritage.* Gibbs Smith.

Wilson, S. (2016). The Philadelphia Centennial Exposition. The Pennsylvania Magazine of History and Biography, 140(3), 363-369.

Wilson, S. (2016). The World's Columbian Exposition: A Centennial Bibliographic Guide. The Pennsylvania Magazine of History and Biography, 140(3), 363-369.

Windschuttle, K. (2009). *The Killing of History.* Free Press.

World Coal Association. (2023). Coal & Electricity. Retrieved from https://www.worldcoal.org/coal/uses-coal/coal-electricity/

Battery & Washington circa 1856: https://cand.uscourts.gov/about/northern-district-history/

Boiler Annex on 1894 Diagram - http://www.sanfranciscomemories.com/mwf/map.html

Calvary Presbyterian Church -
    https://upload.wikimedia.org/wikipedia/commons/thumb/b/b6/Calvary_Presbyterian_%28San_Fra
    ncisco%2C_California%29_3.JPG/1200px-
    Calvary_Presbyterian_%28San_Francisco%2C_California%29_3.JPG

Centennial Exposition of 1876 - https://collaborativehistory.gse.upenn.edu/stories/centennial-
    exposition-1876-evolving-cultural-landscape

Centennial Exposition Of 1876 - https://www.lcpimages.org/centennial/

Central Tower Post Card - https://www.legendsofamerica.com/wp-
    content/uploads/2019/07/CallBldgSpreckelsRotisserie1903.jpg

Chicago Aerial View, 1893 -
    https://en.wikipedia.org/wiki/World%27s_Columbian_Exposition#/media/File:Weltausstellung-
    chicago_brockhaus.jpg

Corliss Engine, Main Exhibition Building - https://digital.hagley.org/AVD_2003_255

Court of Honor, 1894 - https://s.hdnux.com/photos/42/70/50/9144853/5/rawImage.jpg

Crystal Palace 1851 -
    https://images.fastcompany.net/image/upload/w_596,c_limit,q_auto:best,f_auto/fc/3026905-
    inline-i-crystalpalace.jpg

Crystal Palace Interior, 1851 -
    https://en.wikipedia.org/wiki/Great_Exhibition#/media/File:Crystal_Palace_-
    _Queen_Victoria_opens_the_Great_Exhibition.jpg

Crystal Palace, Egyptian Court, 1851 - https://branchcollective.org/?attachment_id=1142

Dickinson's Comprehensive Pictures of the Great Exhibition of 1851 – 1 - https://www.bl.uk/victorian-
    britain/articles/the-great-exhibition

Dickinson's Comprehensive Pictures of the Great Exhibition of 1851 – 2 - https://www.bl.uk/victorian-
    britain/articles/the-great-exhibition

Dillon, R. H. (1983). *The Hatchet Men: The Story of the Tong Wars in San Francisco's Chinatown*. New
    York: Jameson Books.

Electric Tower and Grand Court, C.M.I.E., San Francisco -
    https://oac.cdlib.org/ark:/13030/tf6290119k/?brand=oac4

Electric Tower at Night, C.M.I.E., 1894 - https://oac.cdlib.org/ark:/13030/tf6f59p64x/?brand=oac4

Electrical Tower at Night - https://opensfhistory.org/Download/wnp15.088.jpg

English Bond: https://civilengineeringx.com/super-structures/brick-masonry/

Exposition Universelle of 1867 -
    https://en.wikipedia.org/wiki/Exposition_Universelle_(1867)#/media/File:Vue_officielle_a_vol_d'oi
    seau_de_l'exposition_universelle_de_1867.jpg

EVIDENCE OF THE OLD WORLD

Exposition Universelle of 1867 - https://www.lesmaconsparisiens.fr/histoire/les-expositions-universelles-a-paris/

Fine Arts Building at 1894 - https://www.sanfranciscostory.com/10-highlights-1894-fair/

Fine Arts Building during Midwinter Fair, 1894 - https://www.opensfhistory.org/Display/wnp37.03168.jpg

Flemish Bond: https://civilengineeringx.com/super-structures/brick-masonry/

Flood Building - http://www.ksdgroup.com/flood-building---san-francisco.html

Flood Building Interior, Modern - https://images.squarespace-cdn.com/content/v1/56216cbbe4b0007a00024dd7/1618873362451-QPU2QFALZP6ZNQH3OY2K/hallway-2021.jpg

Flood Building, Modern - https://www.argcs.com/wp-content/uploads/2017/03/Flood-Building_featured.jpg

Fort Jefferson (Third System Architecture): https://www.floridarambler.com/florida-camping/fort-jefferson-dry-tortugas-national-park/

Fort Morgan Interior - https://www.expedia.com/pictures/baldwin-county/gulf-shores/fort-morgan.d6070623

Fort Morgan Interior (Third System Masonry): https://southernresorts.com/blog/a-guide-to-the-history-of-fort-morgan

Fort Morgan LOC: https://www.loc.gov/resource/hhh.al0013.photos/?sp=1

Fort Morgan, Alabama - https://elements.envato.com/fort-morgan-alabama-F8U63JA

Fort Point Interior 2: https://www.presidio.gov/places/fort-point-national-historic-site

Fort Point Interior: https://www.flickr.com/photos/harold_davis/2661907559/

Fort Point with Golden Gate Bridge built over top of it, 1960s: *Fort Point with Golden Gate Bridge built over top of it, 1960s*

Fort Pulaski Interior (Third System Masonry): https://i0.wp.com/www.traveltheparks.com/wp-content/uploads/2022/12/Fort-Pulaski-Southwest-Bastion-WM-650-C.jpg?w=650&ssl=1

Fortification Village of Bourtange - https://elements.envato.com/aerial-view-of-fortification-village-of-bourtange-CNTJJHB

Fountain, 1894 - https://www.sanfranciscostory.com/content/images/2022/05/MMTW0899.JPG

Gaines: https://alabamagenealogy.org/wp-content/uploads/2016/07/Fort-Gaines-Plan.jpg.webp

Gaspar de Portolà - https://en.wikipedia.org/wiki/Gaspar_de_Portol%C3%A1#/media/File:Retrat_Gaspar_de_Portol%C3%A0_(Lleida).jpg

Golden Gate Park. Strawberry Hill, Huntington Falls, Sweeny Observatory - https://www.outsidelands.org/sweeney-observatory.php

Google Map of Star Forts - https://www.google.com/maps/d/u/0/viewer?mid=16we-kJiughWh79KFYUoymhfN2bE&ll=27.763638969146598%2C63.85333824999998&z=2

Grace Cathedral, Modern Day, Front - https://en.wikipedia.org/wiki/File:Grace_Cathedral_(2p).jpg

Grading work for the 1894 Fair - https://www.opensfhistory.org/osfhcrucible/2018/08/26/midwinter-fair-dedication-a-closer-look/

Grand Basin of the 1893 World's Columbian Exposition - https://en.wikipedia.org/wiki/World%27s_Columbian_Exposition#/media/File:Looking_West_From_Peristyle,_Court_of_Honor_and_Grand_Basin,_1893.jpg

Grand Victoria and Palace Hotel (Right) - https://www.foundsf.org/images/thumb/a/a4/Grand_Victoria_and_Palace_Hotels_c_1880s.jpg/800px-Grand_Victoria_and_Palace_Hotels_c_1880s.jpg

Handmade Bricks, Stacked. Modern: https://elements.envato.com/photos/similar-to-KGTX5KE

Hibernia Bank Building, Interior - https://www.structuremag.org/wp-content/uploads/2018/02/0318-bank-2.jpg

Hibernia Bank Building, Modern - https://en.wikipedia.org/wiki/File:2017_Hibernia_Bank_1_Jones_Street.jpg

Horticulture and Agriculture Building, night - https://calisphere.org/item/ark:/13030/tf687011s4/

HV-5 from 1856 - https://www.foundsf.org/index.php?title=WASHERWOMAN%27S_LAGOON

Interior of Fine Arts Building, C.M.I.E., 1894 - https://calisphere.org/item/ark:/13030/tf687011s4/

Issel, W., & Cherny, R. (1986). *San Francisco, 1865-1932: Politics, Power, and Urban Development*. Berkeley: University of California Press.

Italian Exhibits, in Manufacturers' Building, C.M.I.E. - https://calisphere.org/item/ark:/13030/tf687011s4/

James C. Flood Mansion Steps, Modern - https://es.wikipedia.org/wiki/Archivo:James_C._Flood_Mansion_Entrance.JPG

James C. Flood Mansion, Modern - https://es.wikipedia.org/wiki/Archivo:James_Flood_Mansion_(San_Francisco)_4.JPG

John Whites Map - https://www.dncr.nc.gov/blog/2016/04/27/first-roanoke-colonies

Lake below Strawberry Hill, 1894 - https://www.foundsf.org/index.php?title=California_Midwinter_Fair_of_1894:_An_Orientalist_Exposition

Lewis & Clark Continental Map - https://collections.library.yale.edu/catalog/2012144

Lewis & Clark Map - https://collections.library.yale.edu/catalog/2002497

Lotchin, R. W. (2003). *San Francisco, 1846-1856: From Hamlet to City*. Urbana: University of Illinois Press.

Louisiana Map LOC - https://www.loc.gov/resource/g3701sm.gct00482/?sp=21

EVIDENCE OF THE OLD WORLD

MacMonnies Fountain and Machinery Hall, 1893 - https://www.britannica.com/event/Worlds-Columbian-Exposition

Macon NC: https://northcarolinahistory.org/encyclopedia/fort-macon/

Manmade Lake, 1894 - https://opensfhistory.org/Download/wnp24.257a.jpg

Manufactures and Liberal Arts building and the Electric Fountain - https://www.outsidelands.org/court_of_honor.php

Mechanical Arts Building on right, 1894 - https://www.outsidelands.org/opening_midwinter_fair.php

Mechanical Arts Building viewed from Bonet's Electric Tower, 1894 - https://www.outsidelands.org/mechanical_arts_building.php

Mechanical Arts Building, 1894 – https://www.outsidelands.org/court_of_honor.php

Mechanical Arts Building, 1894 - https://www.outsidelands.org/mechanical_arts_building.php

Mechanics' Institute Building - https://www.milibrary.org/sites/default/files/about/31-post-ext.jpg

Modern Brick Pallets: https://elements.envato.com/photos/similar-to-KGTX5KE

Newspaper Row, Central Tower on Right - https://upload.wikimedia.org/wikipedia/commons/thumb/8/82/Newspaper_Row%2C_San_Francisco%2C_Calif._LCCN96510162.jpg/1280px-Newspaper_Row%2C_San_Francisco%2C_Calif._LCCN96510162.jpg

Old City Hall 1856: https://www.cschs.org/history/historic-sites/

Old Custom House circa 1855: https://opensfhistory.org/Display/wnp71.1000.jpg

Old Saint Mary's Cathedral, Interior - https://i0.wp.com/www.cincinnatioratory.com/wp-content/uploads/IMG_3395-scaled.jpg?fit=1600%2C1200&ssl=1

Old Saint Mary's Cathedral, Modern - https://sfcityguides.org/wp-content/uploads/2019/06/SOMA_Yerba_Buena_Starting_Point.jpg

Old U.S. Mint (Mint Plaza), 1874 - https://upload.wikimedia.org/wikipedia/commons/5/5f/Old_San_Francisco_Mint.jpg

Original Sphinx, Fine Arts Building, 1894 - https://www.artandarchitecture-sf.com/wp-content/uploads/2012/02/sphinx.jpg

Palace Hotel Courtyard - https://www.foundsf.org/images/thumb/f/f2/PH_02_725.jpg/720px-PH_02_725.jpg

Panoramic view of the 1878 World Fair - https://repository.library.brown.edu/studio/item/bdr:86964/

Pulaski 1924: https://www.savannah.com/wp-content/uploads/Fort-Pulaski-in-1924.jpg

San Francisco 1850 (Notice already a lot of brick buildings): https://calisphere.org/item/aa856e567821031159e8da60c81a6211/

San Francisco 1853: https://www.maritimeheritage.org/vips/Madam-Pfeiffer.html

San Francisco 1856: https://opensfhistory.org/NeighborhoodPhotos/ALL/skyline

San Francisco Bay looking east - https://elements.envato.com/famous-golden-gate-bridge-san-francisco-usa-ALKZ73J

San Francisco Docks, 1850: https://mua.apps.uri.edu/in_the_field/jd1.shtml

Sansome & Washington circa 1858: https://opensfhistory.org/NeighborhoodPhotos/ALL/government

Smokestacks behind Mechanical Building, 1984 - https://www.outsidelands.org/Image/700/wnp15.128.jpg

St. Francis Hotel, Modern - https://upload.wikimedia.org/wikipedia/commons/thumb/c/c0/Westin_st_francis_san_francisco.jpg/1024px-Westin_st_francis_san_francisco.jpg

Stretcher Bond: https://civilengineeringx.com/super-structures/brick-masonry/

Sumter LOC: https://tile.loc.gov/image-services/iiif/service:gmd:gmd391:g3914:g3914c:cw0387000/full/pct:12.5/0/default.jpg

Temple Emanu-El on Sutter Street - https://www.foundsf.org/images/1/16/Temple_Emanuel_1867_AAB-1709.jpg

Temple Emanu-El on Sutter Street, Interior - https://www.sanfranciscostory.com/content/images/2022/10/synagogue-interior.jpg

The Baldwin from Market Street - https://1.bp.blogspot.com/-cGu5bNlf1Qo/Wnp4bh88u1I/AAAAAAAAa4o/7qzZF03SVAoBsL1rqD9Y0TisW04XGNFDQCLcBGAs/s1600/Baldwin-Hall-c1890.jpg

The Baldwin Hotel - https://i.pinimg.com/originals/16/0f/df/160fdf4e71cb427256047d9b4e63bed7.jpg

The Baldwin Theatre - https://2.bp.blogspot.com/-wfO-ivWve7k/Wnu147NDtmI/AAAAAAAAa8E/K-TR8z1u16gG1Fv2JUbjNtuCfFW7TkCywCEwYBhgL/s1600/Baldwin-Tillmany-DiningRm.jpg

The Bar of the original Palace Hotel - https://en.wikipedia.org/wiki/Palace_Hotel,_San_Francisco#/media/File:Palace_Hotel_Bar_c1895.jpg

The Crystal Palace, 1851 - https://upload.wikimedia.org/wikipedia/commons/9/92/Crystal_Palace_from_the_northeast_from_Dickinson%27s_Comprehensive_Pictures_of_the_Great_Exhibition_of_1851._1854.jpg

The Mark Hopkins Mansion - https://en.m.wikipedia.org/wiki/File:Mark_Hopkins_mansion.jpg

The Mark Hopkins Mansion, Interior - http://1889victorianrestoration.blogspot.com/2011/11/mark-hopkins-mansion.html

The Palace Hotel, 1875 - https://thepalacehotel.org/images725/PH_01_725.jpg

The Parrott Building - https://noehill.com/sf/landmarks/cal0089.asp#:~:text=The%20Parrott%20Block%20was%20erected,soon%20thereafter%20reopened%20for%20business.

Third System Design – Form over Function: https://www.minecreek.info/coastal-fortifications/the-third-system-of-coastal-fortification.html

EVIDENCE OF THE OLD WORLD

Typvs Orbis Terrarvm 1570 - https://www.loc.gov/resource/g3200m.gct00126/?sp=12&r=0.189,0.178,0.112

U.S. Government Building - https://www.britannica.com/event/Worlds-Columbian-Exposition

Urbano Monte's 1587 Map - https://3.bp.blogspot.com/-uYu3_wEt-Xo/XJ_BmxnV8DI/AAAAAAAAD8o/fvulO8Bc-zkQyg-FjJkF97lglqHozYzlACLcBGAs/s1600/res%2Bglobe%2Bnew.jpg

View from Sansome Street 1858- https://cand.uscourts.gov/about/northern-district-history/

View from Woman's Building, World's Columbian Exposition, 1893 - https://daily.jstor.org/the-worlds-fair-that-ignored-more-than-half-the-world/

Vintage Illustration of Midwinter Exposition, 1894 - https://www.atlasobscura.com/places/site-of-the-1894-california-midwinter-international-exposition